Malvinas:

The Argentine perspective of the

Falkland's conflict

A Monograph
by
MAJ Leonardo Arcadio Zarza
Argentine Army

School of Advanced Military Studies
United States Army Command and General Staff College
Fort Leavenworth, Kansas

AY 09-10

Approved for Public Release; Distribution is Unlimited

Abstract

MALVINAS: THE ARGENTINE PERSPECTIVE OF THE FALKLANDS CONFLICT by MAJOR Leonardo Arcadio Zarza, Argentine Army, 61 pages.

This monograph addresses the Malvinas/Falklands conflict from the Argentine perspective. Leaders must understand all sides of narratives in order to frame the right problem in armed conflicts. Existing Anglo-American literature does not reflect the complete narrative associated with the conflict. This does not mean that what has been written is not true, but that the Argentine view has not been captured effectively. This conflict escalated into war between Argentina and Great Britain between April and June of 1982, but the outcome of that war did not solve the problem.

The author is an Argentine Army Aviator Officer who wants to take a balanced and objective view. The Anglo-American view interprets the Argentine behavior as an invasion, the Argentines' view is perceived as a recovery of the Islands without bloodshed after 149 years of persistent claims. From the Argentine view the war was triggered by Great Britain with the British decision to sink the Argentine cruiser *General Belgrano* on 2nd May 1982, outside of the theater of operations, causing the deaths of more than three hundred Argentine sailors. Until that point in the conflict, Great Britain had suffered no casualties in the Argentine recovery of the Islands.

The Malvinas/Falklands conflict includes issues about sovereignty, colonialism, and diplomatic misunderstandings. If the conflict reignites, it has the propensity and the potentiality to transmit the issues latent in the Argentine domestic conflict to the entire South American region, acting against the interests of the United States and the values of partnership in the international community.

TABLE OF CONTENTS

Glossary 4
Section 1: Introduction... 5
Section 2: The Facts... 9
    Negotiations and United Nations resolutions.. 13
    The Road to War... 14
    Landing and Argentine occupation 14
    End of the military battles - but the conflict still goes on 20
Section 3: The British perspective 22
    British Diplomacy - British Rights and Legitimacy over the Islands 24
    British Self- Determination 26
Section 4: The Argentine perspective 28
    Sovereignty 28
    Diplomacy... 30
    The Argentine Recovery Campaign: Operation Virgin del Rosario 32
    The Argentine Defense Campaign 33
    Argentine popular view... 37
    The legal Perspective: Malvinas in the Argentine National Constitution 39
    Colonialism... 40
Section 5: Conclusions... 43
    British perspective 43
    Argentine Perspective 44
    The way ahead 45
Appendix I: Argentine Map of the Malvinas Islands... 47
Appendix II: Relative Location of the Malvinas 48
Appendix III: Surrender Document 49
Appendix IV– Different Perceptions of the Malvinas Conflict 50
Appendix V: Falklands Observed System - British Perspective.. 51
Appendix VI: System Propensity... 52
Appendix VII: System Potential (with Intervention). 53
Appendix VIII: Observed System- Argentine Perspective 54
Appendix IX: Tensions 55
Appendix X: Desired System... 56
Bibliography 57

Glossary

ARA: Armada Argentina (Argentine Navy)

DENAC: Argentine National Strategy Directive

DEMIL: Argentine Military Strategy Directive

EU: European Union

FAS: Argentine Air Force South

Isla Soledad: East Falkland Island

Isla Gran Malvina: West Falkland Island

Isla Georgias: South Georgia Island

Malvinas: Called "The Falklands" by Great Britain

MERCOSUR: South American Common Market

NATO: North Atlantic Treaty Organization

Puerto Argentino: Capital of Malvinas (Called Port Stanley by Great Britain)

TOAS: Argentine Theater of Operations South Atlantic

TOM: Theater of Operations Malvinas

UNASUR: Union of South American Nations

VGM: Argentine Veteran from Malvinas War

Section 1: Introduction

History knows no laws.
But it does teach lessons,
at least those of warnings.[1]

In April 1982, after 149 years of unsuccessful diplomatic protests, Argentina decided to recover the Malvinas/Falklands, Georgias and South Sandwich Islands. The Argentine Armada (ARA) Carrier *25 de Mayo* and four more Argentine vessels covered the destroyer *Santisima Trinidad*, the ARA Icebreaker *Admiral Irizar*, the ARA *Transport Cabo San Antonio*, and ARA submarine *Santa Fe, as they* pushed south through the windy and cold waters of the Argentine Sea. On board was the Argentine Joint Task Force for the military Operation *Virgin del Rosario*. On April 1, at 0345hs, the Argentine Marines landed in Faro San Felipe on the east of Soledad Island (East Falkland).[2]

The Argentine Marine Commander, Captain Pedro Giachino, was told by his superior that he was to accomplish his mission in such a way that: "Neither British military nor local civilians should be killed during the entire Argentine military operation over own territory."[3] Giachino knew that that mission went beyond the simple seizure of territory and that any loss of life would hurt the post-war negotiations that were sure to follow. Confronting British Royal Marines defending the British Governor's house on 2 April, he was shot trying to get the British to lay down their arms. Shortly after, the British Governor in Port Argentino (Port Stanley) surrendered and at 1230, the Argentine Flag flew over the Malvinas/Falklands for the first time since 1833. The Argentine military accomplished its task without British casualties.

---

[1] Barry, Gough, *The Falkland Islands/Malvinas: The contest for Empire in the South Atlantic* (London: Atlantic Highlands, NJ: Athlone Press, 1992), 159.

[2] Carlos, Landaburu, *La Guerra de las Malvinas:Historical background of the Malvinas Conflict.* (Buenos Aires-Argentina: Circulo Militar, 1989), 121.

[3] Argentine Army, *Informe Oficial del Ejercito Argentino Tomo II -Conflicto Malvinas (*Buenos Aires-Argentina: Estado Mayor General del Ejercito Argentino 1983): Annex 6.

Today, Captain Giachino is an Argentine national hero. The numerous events of the war, both good and bad, form a narrative of the conflict fundamentally different from that understood in most English speaking countries. The conventional war, fought from April 2 until June 14 1982, resulted from disagreements and misunderstandings over the *Malvinas/Falklands* Islands by both sides. The cease-fire terms were only partially satisfactory.[4] The fact that the disputed islands are still in the news in 2010 indicates just how problematic the settlement was.

However, more important for the purposes of this monograph, is why each nation views the events of those days differently. Each side has a different narrative, or way a viewing its placing its history in context. To be fair and honest with the learning process, most of the Argentine narrative has not been captured effectively sometimes just because the books are in Spanish and they did not reach the English audience. The word "Malvinas" or "Falklands" by itself gives the meaning and the metaphor in which each audience live by.

Narratives are important because they translate knowing into telling. The Argentine narrative has been told but only created "meaning" for the Argentine, Spanish and South American audience. Historic narratives try to be objective but the discourse tends to be subjective. Each state has its own narrative discourse and the influence of the latter brings more subjectivity to the real story causing a distortion in the perception of the Malvinas conflict. The challenge is to discover the real story behind the Falklands conflict.[5]

Narratives are also important, especially in representation of reality of the sort embodied in historical discourse. According to Hayden White, "narrativizing discourse serves the purpose of moralizing judgments. The discourse is the process of comparing/contrasting competing narratives in order to gain shared understanding. It is not a debate where British and Argentines try to convince each

---

[4] Argentine Army. *Informe Oficial del Ejercito Argentino Tomo II -Conflicto Malvinas (*Buenos Aires-Argentina: Estado Mayor General del Ejercito Argentino 1983): Annex 79. See Appendix III.

[5] Hayden, White. *The Content of the Form-Narrative, discourse and historical representation*, (Baltimore and London, Johns Hopkins University Press, 1987) 1-5.

other of their personal narrative, but to try to discover the truth by exploring different perspectives." [6] The other face of narratives is the politics of historical interpretation; this should be disciplined and de-sublimated. According to Clausewitz's, the balancing forces between government, military and the people, are driven by this interpretation.[7] This interpretation gets in the way of understanding and diplomacy and can form the foundations of how the passion of the people is developed, fired up, and restrained. This different narrative, interpretations frame " perceptions" that continues to linger like a virus, especially in protracted conflicts like Malvinas, infecting everything around it and causing "crisis" to pop up from time to time.

Understanding the importance of narratives and these different perceptions raises the question: How does the Argentine perspective on the Malvinas/Falklands War differ from the current Anglo-American perspective? While the two narratives agree on many of the facts surrounding this conflict, the British narrative contains a focus on self-determination, right of discovery and effective occupation. The thesis that the author sustains is that the Argentine perspective of the 1982 Malvinas/Falklands War includes diplomatic misunderstandings, sovereignty issues, and colonial concerns heretofore that have been either overlooked or underemphasized. The Argentine view is but one of several views that need explanation in order to understand fully the conflict's meaning and impact. For Argentina, the war did not solve the political conflict around Malvinas/Falklands. The challenge for soldiers and diplomats from both countries is how to address these differing perspectives.

The other aspect of the problem is about the role of the United Nations as a key player in the international organization system. The United Nations could not enforce the resolutions requiring a dialogue about Sovereignty between Argentina and Great Britain. These actions exposed a weakness in the United Nations system and led to a lack of credibility for the organization.

---

[6] Ibid., 24, 58.

[7] Carl Von Clausewitz, *On War* (New Jersey, Princeton University Press, 1984), 30.

This monograph considers not only the standard literature from the Anglo-American community but also the rich and often seen as contentious sources in Argentina. Anglo-American literature includes: Freedman and Lawrence's *The Official history of the Falklands campaign.* Others are: Max Hastings and Simon Jenkins with their book: *The Battle for the Falklands,* which is almost accurate and balanced in their view of the conflict and good quality. Also expressing the Anglo-American viewpoint is Gough and Barry's *The Falkland Islands/Malvinas The contest for Empire in the South Atlantic,* andJames Aulich's *Framing the Falklands War: Nationhood, Culture, and Identity.* Badsey, Havers and Grove's *The Falklands Conflict twenty years on: lessons for the future,* addressed the conflict in 292 pages but dedicates only three pages to an Argentine view. Other British sources are Dorman, Andrew and Kennedy in *War and Diplomacy: From World War I to the War on Terrorism*; Anderson's *The Falklands War, 1982*; Nora Femenia's *National Identity in times of crisis: the scripts of the Falklands-Malvinas War*; and Julian Thompson's *No Picnic*. These are just a few of the many great books on the Falklands Campaign, but they minimize the Argentine perspective on the War.[8]

In Argentina, the national perspective is dominated by the Argentine official publication called *Malvinas: Informe Rattenbach.*and the Argentine Army's *Informe Oficial del Ejercito Argentino Tomo I and II -Conflicto Malvinas..* In addition, this monograph has mined the wide array of literate available including *The History of the South Atlantic Conflict: The War for the Malvinas* written by Ruben Moro, which is the source from the Argentine Air Force among others. Other important Argentine sources in general are: Carlos Landaburu's *La Guerra de las Malvinas: Historical background of the Malvinas Conflict;* Aguiar and Cervo's *Land Operations in Malvinas*; Graciela Corizzo's *Conflicts in the South Atlantic*; and Martin Balza's, *Asi peleamos Malvinas: Testimonios de veteranos del Ejercito,* and *Malvinas: Relatos de Soldados.* An important source that address the Argentine commando operations was the book written by Isidoro Ruiz Moreno: *Comandos en Accion.* Munoz, Chacho, and Garasino's *Malvinas; Album de Campana;* Nora Stewart's *Mates y muchachos: Unity cohesion in the*

---

[8] Full citation for these British sources is presented in the bibliography.

Falklands/Malvinas War; and *Operaciones terrestres en las Islas Malvinas* published by the Argentine Circulo Militar, all address the conflict from the Argentine view.[9]

Narratives frame perceptions and perceptions frame realities. According to FM 3-24 *Counterinsurgency*, narrative is "the central mechanism, expressed in story form, through which ideologies are expressed and absorbed."[10] British, American, and Argentine officers have a long and important history of cooperation and mutual support. In politically charged environments, it is the professionalism of the officer that can make the difference between needless war and protracted but peaceful negotiations. The goal of this monograph is to further this process.

Section 2: The Facts

The World is not run by those who are right;
it is run by those who can convince others
that they are right.[11]

Barry Gough includes in his book *The Falkland Islands/Malvinas* preface: "that a War is waged to the present day as to which is the correct name to give these islands is symbolic of the larger question of the disputed sovereignty of the archipelago."[12] However, while there are issues in dispute, there are many elements that both perspectives agree on.

The presumed discovery of the Islands has been attributed to, among others, Americo Vespucio in 1502 in the service of Portugal, and the Spaniard Hernando de Magallanes in 1520. The islands are

---

[9] Full citation for these Argentine sources is presented in the bibliography.

[10] FM 3-24 *Counterinsurgency* (Headquarters Department of the United States Army, Dec 2006), Glossary-6.

[11] Jamshid Gharajedaghi, Systems Thinking: Managing Chaos and Complexity: A platform for Designing Business Architecture, (New York –London, 2006), 34.

[12] Barry, Gough, *The Falkland Islands/Malvinas: The contest for Empire in the South Atlantic* (The Athlone Press-London and AtlanticHighlands, NJ, 1992), xii.

registered in the following documents: the map of Spaniard Pedro Reniel (1523), the map of Weiner (1527), a map of the world by Diego de Ribeiro (1529), Islands of the world by Alonso Santa Cruz (1541), and a map from Sebastian Gaboto (1544). In 1670, Great Britain intended to occupy Port Deseado, in what is today Patagonia, Argentina, but the local population rejected the British overtures.[13] In 1806, there was another encounter in Buenos Aires, but the local militias from the United Provinces of the River Plate repulsed the British attack. The second defense of Buenos Aires took place in 1807. The result was the Argentine revolution on 25 May 1810.[14] Argentina separated from Spain, declared its independence, and created the new Argentine Army on 29 May in order to protect themselves from further attacks.

For the British, the Malvinas Island's first recorded sighting was August 14 1592 by the English sea captain John Davis in the ship *Desire.* The first recorded landing was in 1690 by the English navigator John Strong in his ship *Welfare*. He named the channel dividing the two main islands Falkland Sound after Viscount Falkland, then treasurer of the Royal Navy. Over the years several French ships visited the Islands, which they called *Les Iles Malouines* after the French port of Saint Malo. In 1765, unaware of the French settlement, Commodore John Byron landed at Port Egmont and took the Islands for the British Crown. In 1774, Great Britain withdrew from Port Egmont on economic grounds as part of a redeployment of forces due to unrest in the American colonies, which would eventually escalate into its War of Independence. In 1816 the United Provinces of the River Plate declared independence from Spain, becoming what is today the Argentine Republic, exercising sovereignty over *Malvinas/Falklands* until 1833.[15]

---

[13] Graciela Corizzo, Conflicts in the South Atlantic: The unfortunate usurpation of Port Deseado (Buenos Aires-Argentina: Circulo Militar, 1988), 20

[14] Ibid., 25.

[15] Government of the Falkland Islands, http:// www.falklands.gov.fk/historical-Data.html, accessed 12/28/2009.

From 1492 until 1810 Spain and Portugal were the main maritime and imperial powers in South America. Great Britain and France were more influential after 1810.[16] Problems arose when Napoleon invaded Spain in 1805. Great Britain responded with its maritime power and its actions had repercussions in the Spanish South Atlantic colonies. Moreover, the political ideals of the French Revolution manifested in the ideas of liberty, fraternity and equality would also influence future South American political development. Occupied Spain tried to resist Napoleonic forces but it could not protect its colonies. This left its South American possessions such as the Viceroyalty of Rio de la Plata, to its own resources and without military protection.

Spain had exercised sovereignty over the Malvinas Islands since their discovery. The British were granted only temporary dispositions to trade, hunt, and fish following the Nootka Sound (Canada) convention in 1790. By this convention, Great Britain also renounced its intentions to colonize any territory in South America.[17] Between 1765 and 1770, there was a British presence in Port Egmont[18] along with Spanish and French settlements. Spain ruled the islands as part of the Viceroyalty of Peru until 1776. They then became part of the Viceroyalty of River Plate for more than 55 years until 1810 when the Spanish withdrew the garrison because of the Argentine war for independence.[19]

Argentina exercised administrative sovereignty rights over the Malvinas after 1810. After Argentine independence in 1816, United States-born Captain David Jewett commanding the Argentine Frigate *Heroina* formally installed Argentine rule over the islands in 1820.[20] For thirteen years, Argentina

---

[16] Carlos Landaburu, *La Guerra de las Malvinas:Historical background of the Malvinas Conflict.* (Buenos Aires-Argentina: Circulo Militar, 1989), 19-20.

[17] Graciela Corizzo, *Conflicts in the South Atlantic: The unfortunate usurpation of Port Deseado* (Buenos Aires-Argentina: Circulo Militar, 1988), 15 and Nootka Sound Convention article 6.

[18] Carlos Landaburu, *La Guerra de las Malvinas: Historical background of the Malvinas Conflict* (Buenos Aires-Argentina: Circulo Militar, 1988), 21. Port Egmond was a part of the Malvinas/Falkland Islands where Spain authorized British settlements around 1770 for trade fishing and hunting purposes and as a key port to use as a maritime power, between the Atlantic and the Pacific.

[19] Sergio Fernandez, Malvinas 1982: Symmetrical Misunderstandings and Overreactions Lead the Way to War (United States Army War College, 2002), 3.

[20] Ibid. Colonel David Jewet was an United States-born Captain in service with the Argentine Navy. He took possession of the Malvinas Islands for the United Provinces in Port Soledad, November 6, 1820 in presence of

effectively ruled the islands, despite the attack and the destruction of the Argentine settlement in 1831 by the frigate USS *Lexington*, acting in reprisal for the Argentine imprisonment of American seamen who were illegally fishing in the islands.[21] By 1833, Malvinas Islands were part of the Viceroyalty of the Rio de la Plata. On January 3, 1833, the British invaded the Islands with two warships, the HMS *Tyne* and *Clio*, under the command of Captain James Oslow, and the Islands became a colony of Britain.[22] They forcibly removed the Argentine population that had been living in the islands for 23 years.[23]

The dispute over the Georgias and Sandwich Islands evolved differently. In 1908, the British government made an administrative internal letter patent in relation to the overseas territories, supported again by military power. By this patent, Great Britain's crown claimed all the Argentine and Chilean islands associated with the Argentine mainland, except Tierra del Fuego. It took Argentina nine years to obtain a partial rectification of this fraudulent claim.[24] With the opening of the Panama Canal in August 1914, there was another priority given to the Malvinas Islands by Great Britain. Before the Panama Canal, it was the key port from the Atlantic to the Pacific. After the Canal opened, it became the lynchpin for British interests in Antarctica and its associated natural resources.[25]

Finally, all of these factors about rights of discovery, settlement, occupation and competing claims over the Malvinas conditioned the Argentina's behavior in World War I and II. When Argentina was invited to participate in World War I as an ally of Great Britain, Argentine President Roque Saenz

---

about 50 fishing and whaling ships, among them British (6) and American (6). The information was published, among others, by the Salem Gazette (US) and the Redactor from Cadiz (Spain).

[21] Max Hastings and Simon Jenkins. The Battle for the Falklands. (New York-London: WW Norton and Company, 1983), 5: Hasting and Jenkins stated "If any action in history can be said to have been the cause of the 1982 Falklands War, it was taken by the reckless captain of USS Lexington, Captain Silas Duncan, on arrival at Puerto Soledad. He not only recovered the confiscated Sealskins, but also spiked the Argentine guns, blew up their powder, sacked the settlement buildings and arrested most of the inhabitants. He then declared the islands free of all government and sailed away. His action was pure piracy."

[22] Robert Love, *History of the United States Navy* Volume One 1775-1941(Harrisburg: Stackpole Books, 1992), 159. Goebel, Julius, *The Struggle for the Falklands* (New Haven: Yale University Press, 1982), 438.

[23] Sergio Fernandez, Malvinas 1982: Symmetrical Misunderstandings and Overreactions Lead the Way to war, (United States Army War College, 2002), 3 and 43.

[24] Ibid., 5.

[25] Carlos Landaburu, *La Guerra de las Malvinas* (Buenos Aires-Argentina: Circulo Militar, 1989), 45.

Pena's response was: "First return the Malvinas, then we can talk."Caused by this situation about the sovereignty of Malvinas dispute, the same behavior came out in World War II.[26]

Negotiations and United Nations resolutions

In 1964, the United Nations tried to solve the Malvinas, Georgias, and South Sandwich Islands sovereignty issue for the first time. Negotiations in the United Nations were undertaken between Argentina and Great Britain, but progress was halted due to British disinterest. In 1968, British lobbying against the process of negotiations with Argentina was effective, so the British Foreign office withdraw the proposal to negotiate over sovereignty. The subsequent 37 years have yielded no significant progress. United Nation's Resolution 2353 of 1968, for a similar case involving British-Spanish relations over the British overseas territory of Gibraltar, expressed clearly that "*any colonial situation which partially or completely destroys the national unity and territorial integrity of a country is incompatible with the purpose and principles of the Charter of the United Nations.*"[27]

In 1971, the situation improved slightly with communications agreements established between Argentina and Britian, with Argentina beginning to support development in the islands.[28] In 1976, the situation changed substantially as a result of unsuccessful negotiations over oil exploration. In 1977, Great Britain dispatched a nuclear submarine and supporting units to the South Atlantic, facing what Great Britain called Argentine military escalation of the dispute. The lingering misunderstandings and unresolved sovereignty issue created an environment resulting in the lack of international trust between Argentina and Great Britain by the end of 1980, setting the conditions for war.

---

[26] Ibid.

[27] United Nations Resolutions 1514, 2065, 3160, 31/49, 502, 505, 37/9, 38/12, 39/6, 40/21, 41/40, 42/19, and 43/25.

[28] By this time Argentina operated routinely airlines called LADE (Lineas Aereas del Estado=Argentine States Airlines) between the Malvinas and the Argentine mainland.

The Road to War

Between 26 and 27 February 1982, the sixth round of negotiations between Argentina and Great Britain took place at United Nations headquarters in New York. The meeting attempted to find a final resolution to the Malvinas dispute, but negotiations failed to make any progress whatsoever. This new failure caused a great frustration in the Argentine ministry of foreign affairs and in the wider government. On March 1, 1982, the Argentine government issued a public statement that declared that it had decided that Argentina was free to choose the best course of action in moving forward in the Malvinas dispute, and would do so according to Argentine national interests.

In response, Great Britain delivered an ultimatum to the Argentine Government over the presence of Argentine workers in a factory in San Pedro in the Georgias Islands, who were flying the Argentine flag. Great Britain requested that Argentina repatriate the workers, as they were working illegally under British law.[29] Argentina's answer to Great Britain was that the workers were indeed legally authorized to work in San Pedro according to an agreement that had been made with British government representatives in Port Argentino (Port Stanley), and that it would protect the rights of the workers. On 30 March 1982, the British Minister for Foreign Affairs asked the British Parliament to reinforce the British military garrison in Malvinas. On April 1, 1982, the Argentina's representative to the United Nations presented a note in the Security Council where it referenced the British reluctance to negotiate sovereignty issues associated with the disputed islands and the threat by the British to use military force to expel the Argentine workers.[30]

Landing and Argentine occupation

The decision to recover the islands by military means surprised not only the British but also the Argentinean people. The Argentinean Minister for Foreign Affairs, Nicanor Costa Mendez, believed that

---

[29] Argentine Army, *Informe Oficial del Ejercito Argentino Tomo I -Conflicto Malvinas (*Buenos Aires-Argentina: Estado Mayor General del Ejercito Argentino 1983), 23.

[30] Ibid., 24.

Argentina's decision would be looked upon favorably by the United Nations and United States. By occupying the Malvinas, so close to Argentina but so far from Great Britain, Argentina would compel Great Britain to negotiate the Malvinas sovereignty issue once and for all, with Argentina able to negotiate from a position of strength.[31]

On April 7, 1982, British Prime Minister Margaret Thatcher decided to launch Operation *Corporate*, the British mission to regain the islands by force, and dispatched a substantial Task Force to the Malvinas Islands.

On April 8, 1982, Argentina established the *Argentine Theater of Operations of South Atlantic* (TOAS), superseding the *Theater of Operations Malvinas* (TOM), in order to change posture from recovery and diplomatic negotiation to the defense of the islands. Also at this time Argentina issued Operations Order 01/81, for the defense of the Malvinas.[32] The plan recognized that Argentina would face some difficulties defending the islands without the development of significant military infrastructure and capabilities in the theatre. The defense plan was received on the 23rd of April 1982 by the Argentine Governor of the Malvinas, General Mario Benjamin Menendez, who was appointed the Argentine Joint Military Commander of the Islands.[33]

The first contact between Argentine and British military forces occurred on April 21, 1982, between an Argentine Boeing 707 conducting a surveillance mission and the British Task Force. On April 26, British forces conducted Operation *Paraquat*, landing on and securing South Georgia Island while diplomatic negotiations were still ongoing.[34] The Argentinean force on South Georgia surrendered and

---

[31] Roberto Aguiar, *Operaciones terrestres en las Islas Malvinas* (Buenos Aires-Argentina: Circulo Militar, 1985), 25.

[32] Argentine Army. *Informe Oficial del Ejercito Argentino Tomo I -Conflicto Malvinas* (Buenos Aires-Argentina: Estado Mayor General del Ejercito Argentino 1983), 31-37.

[33] Ibid., 32: The South Atlantic Theater of Operations (TOAS) Plan, stated the mission: "consolidate the insular zone, impede the recovery from the opponent and support the military actions, in order to exercise the Argentine sovereignty over the Malvinas, Georgias and Sandwich del Sur Islands, and contribute to assure freedom of action in the South Atlantic."

[34] Bruce Watson and Dunn Peter, *Military lessons of the Falkland Island War: Views From the United States* (Arms and Armor Press, London-England, 1984), 146-149.

the Argentine submarine ARA *Santa Fe* was sunk. The small Argentine Force surrendered in the face of overwhelming British force, cognisant that their mission was only to protect the Argentinean workers on the island, not to fight to defend the terrain. On April 30, the Great Britain declared that a total exclusion zone had come into effect around the Falklands, and United States President Ronald Reagan announced support for Britain in the conflict. On May 1, Britain conducted Operation *Black Buck* 1, the first of seven long-range raids conducted on the islands by Vulcan bombers. On May 2, while Peru and the United Nations were presenting a draft peace plan, the British submarine *Conqueror* sunk the ARA cruiser *General Belgrano* approximately 35 miles south-west of exclusion zone.[35] Argentina responded with its Air Force. On May 4, the British destroyer *Sheffield* was hit by an Exocet missile sinking six days later; on May 12, the destroyer *Glasgow* was damaged by a bomb, forcing its return to Britain; on May 21, the frigate *Ardent* sunk after being struck by several 1,000lb bombs; and on May 25, the destroyer *Coventry* was bombed and British merchant navy ship *Atlantic Conveyor* was struck by Exocet missiles, with the loss of both vessels. On May 6, Great Britain formally accepted the offer of United Nations mediation.[36]

The Argentine defense plan for the two main islands was based on a series of strong points on Soledad Island (East Falkland); primarily at Port Argentino, Darwin, Goose Green, Bahia Fox, and several smaller outposts on Gran Malvina Island (West Falkland). The plan was designed to prevent the encirclement of ground forces, as the British had already established naval and local air superiority. The Argentine military was not prepared to fight Great Britain in a conventional war in the South Atlantic because there was no overall Argentine grand strategy and no campaign plan issued until April 12, 1982.[37]

---

[35] Stephen Badsey, Rob Havers, Mark Grove "*The Falklands conflict twenty years on, lessons for the future*": Admiral Sir John Woodward: A personal view. (Frank Cass London New York, 2005), 4-5.

[36] Ibid.

[37] Argentine Army. *Informe Oficial del Ejercito Argentino Tomo I -Conflicto Malvinas* (Buenos Aires-Argentina: Estado Mayor General del Ejercito Argentino 1983), 29. The Argentine Defense Plan was delivered and improvised during March, without understanding the operational environment after 4 April 1982, where the actors involved were not just Argentina and the United Kingdom. Argentina attempted to feed more forces over to the Islands but did so through improvisation rather than through careful planning. The operational picture, if it was

The Argentine military's strategic objective was to defend Puerto Argentino (Port Stanley), but without local air and naval superiority, and tenuous lines of communications back to the mainland, it was unable to achieve this goal. On May 21, 1982, British amphibious forces from 3 Commando Brigade (approximately 4000 troops from 2nd Parachute Battalion (2 Para), 3rd parachute Battalion (3 Para), 40 Commando , 42 Commando and 45 Commando (Royal Marines)) commenced landing at Port San Carlos, and quickly defeated the small Argentine force defending the area. The Argentinean command and control system faced a dilemma during the British landings at Port San Carlos. There was heated discussion at the highest levels on whether to change the operational objective from defending Port Argentine to defending San Carlos, in order to defeat the British Forces during the landing operations, arguably their point of greatest vulnerability. However, the lack of local air and sea power, the scarcity of logistics, and the 100km distance between the established defensive positions at Port Argentine and Post San Carlos, made any such change extremely risky, if not unfeasible. Unfortunately for the Argentineans, their land force was not designed to defend against such a robust invasion force. The objective of the Argentine occupation force of 2 April was to conduct a "Touch and Go" military Operation, simply to protect Argentine workers and force diplomatic negotiations, not to conduct a deliberate defense against a well-equipped joint force with air and naval superiority.

The British land campaign to recover the islands was conducted in three broad phases: Securing Port San Carlos (British amphibious assault – initial objective), securing Darwin-Goose Green (intermediate objective), and securing in Port Argentino (the final objective and the decisive battle).

After the loss of the *Belgrano,* the Argentina relied exclusively on its Air Force and naval aviation to disrupt the British Navy and prevent British ground forces from landing in the Malvinas. Likewise, Britain relied on its Navy to cut the lines of communication across the Argentine Sea and isolate the Argentine land forces in the Islands. From the start of the San Carlos operation, the British

---

compiled accurately with an adequate intelligence and preparation of the battlefield would show that after 4 April, Argentina would be fighting in the following days the United Kingdom supported by the United States and also Argentina's neighbor Chile.

Royal Navy lost ten ships in three days from attacks by the Argentine Air Force, a figure that could have been larger if the some eighty percent of free-fall bombs that were dropped hadn't malfunctioned due to faulty fusing.[38] The Argentine Air Force also hit and damaged the frigates HMS *Broadsword* and *Brilliant*.[39]

On May 27, 1982, Argentine *Task Force Mercedes* received Operations Order 506/82 for the defense of the Darwin-Goose Green area.[40] This task force was based on the reinforced Infantry Regiment 12, which deployed to Malvinas on May 1, from Corrientes, Argentina. Supporting personnel included elements of the 25th Infantry Regiment, a battery from the 4h Airborne Artillery Group, a platoon of engineers, and an air defense platoon.[41] Lieutenant Colonel Italo Piaggi was the Argentine Commander. His mission was to defend the Darwin-Goose Green airfield. Part of the force was designated as a situational airmobile reserve for the Argentine Joint Command in the Malvinas. *Task Force Mercedes'* scheme of maneuver was to counterattack at selected points on Island Soledad, and was able to delay the advance of the British 2 Para from 27 until 29 May.[42] *Task Force Mercedes* tried valiantly to delay the British advance, with one Rifle Company suffering a fifty percent casualty rate. Isolated from the forces in Port Argentino, and without sufficient air support, *Task Force Mercedes* faced an uphill struggle as Argentine forces desperately lacked ammunition resupply, and were forced to fight with only the ammunition they carried. The British used the night and periods of poor weather and visibility to advance, resting during the day.[43] Part of the 25th Infantry Regiment, led by Argentine

---

[38] Bruce Watson and Dunn Peter, *Military lessons of the Falkland Island War, views from the United States* (Arms and Armor Press, London-England, 1984), 158.

[39] Ibid., 158.

[40] Argentine Army. *Informe Oficial del Ejercito Argentino Tomo I -Conflicto Malvinas.* Buenos Aires-Argentina: Estado Mayor General del Ejercito Argentino 1983), 78-91.

[41] Ibid., 78.

[42] Roberto Aguiar and Franciso Cervo. *Land Operations in Malvinas* (Buenos Aires-Argentina:Circulo Militar, 1985), 179: There were more than ten possible British landing places just in Island Soledad in which this small Task Force had to defend Darwin and also be employed as a joint operational reserve.

[43] Ibid., 165-166.

Lieutenant Roberto Estevez,[44] counterattacked the British forces along one axis of the advance. With a small force, Estevez accomplished part of his mission in delaying elements of 2 Para, but it eventually cost him his life. Although seriously wounded, he directed the Argentine artillery fires and covered the withdrawal of the Argentine force.

The British forces did not achieve their desired breakthrough at Darwin-Goose Green due to what appeared to be a strong Argentine defense around Darwin Hill. The British commander of 2 Para, Lieutenant Colonel Herbert Jones, lost patience and led an assault on Darwin Hill, personally losing his life and eleven of his men. Both sides had heroic leaders like Jones and Estevez, both of whom were killed in action and posthumously earned the highest military honors from their countries, the Victoria Cross and the Argentine Medal to the Valor in Combat.[45] The misunderstandings and protracted costs of the diplomatic arena had moved to the battlefield with a terrible human cost.

Without air superiority and suffering from continuous British artillery bombardment over their frozen positions, the Argentine troops could resist no more. In May 1982, around one hundred and fifty civilians lived in the Darwin-Goose Green area. Argentine commanders wanted to avoid any civilian casualties and attempted to negotiate with the British commanders in order to evacuate civilians. The British answer was negative. This made the Argentine commander responsible for any civilian casualties. With the prospect of serious civilian casualties, and a lack of confidence in Argentine military success in

---

[44] Ruben Moro, The *History of the South Atlantic Conflict-The War for the Malvinas* (New York-Praeger, London, 1989), 260: "Lieutenant Roberto Estevez, who had fewer men than his counterpart blocked British Company B from advancing from the West. Although wounded, he started calling artillery corrections. As he fell mortally wounded, his dying order was to his squad leader to continue the mission. The squad leader was also soon dead, and a private took up the position but was also soon killed in action." Estevez was honored with the highest honor the Argentine government bestows for gallant military actions: "The Heroic Valor in Combat Argentine Medal".

[45] Ibid, 264: Lieutenant Colonel Herbert Jones lost his patience due to several actions. On 28 May, Goose Green Air Base Sector was defended i by Second Lieutenant Gomez Centurion and his platoon. The Lieutenant contacted British forces. At some point during the combat, the British forces started waving their helmets as in a bid for a truce. A British Officer, Lieutenant Jim Barry presented himself and demanded the surrender of the Argentine platoon, to which question the answer from the Argentine officer was: "In two minutes we reopen fire." The British version states that this was a confusing action where the Argentines waved a flag of truce. Further investigations have determined that none of the commanders of the Argentine side had intended to surrender.

the campaign, Lieutenant Colonel Italo Piaggi decided to conclude the Darwin Goose-Green operation.[46] Colonel Felix Roberto Aguiar and Colonel Francisco Cervo were members of the Joint Chief of Staff in Port Argentine during the war and they subsequently analyzed the Battle of Darwin-Goose Green.[47] They concluded that the Argentine forces in the Darwin area of operations, despite having a superior number of troops, were deficient combat power in to their British opponents. Without ammunition resupply there was no possibility of success.[48] Regardless of this analysis, Darwin-Goose Green was not an Argentine failure because the defense was too static, but because it was not synchronized into a coherent operational plan. Even the best tactics rarely solve the problem of having a poor strategy.

Argentina's main effort during the conflict was to try and achieve a favorable diplomatic solution. This was another big Argentinean error. Once at war, military leaders should fight like soldiers, not like diplomats. On June 4 1982, Great Britain vetoed a United Nations Security Council motion calling for ceasefire.[49] It was evident that Great Britain had prioritized war over diplomacy.

End of the military battles - but the conflict still goes on

One week later, following three days of intensive artillery bombardment, the British launched their the final assault of the campaign: the attack on Port Argentine.. On June 11th 1982, a British naval shell struck a civilian house that was thought to be unoccupied. Three female civilians were killed. These were the only civilian fatalities in the entire Falklands Campaign.[50] Despite the lack of support from the British residents, Argentine forces did not kill or seriously injure any civilians during the entire campaign. Three days later, Argentine Governor and commander of the Argentine Forces General Mario Menendez

---

[46] Roberto Aguiar, Francisco Cervo. *Land Operations in Malvinas* (Buenos Aires: Circulo Militar, 1985), 174: "On 29th May of 1982, the commander of the Argentine TF Mercedes arranged a cease fire with Major Keeble, Deputy Commander of the British Forces in Darwin-Goose Green to avoid more unnecessary military and civilian casualties."

[47] Ibid., 155-157. Comparison of Relative Combat Power between Adversaries.

[48] Ibid., 306: Table 1: Indicators to assess Argentine Resistance.

[49] Bruce Watson, and Dunn Peter. *Military lessons of the Falkland Island War, Views from the United States* (Arms and Armor Press, London-England, 1984), 161.

[50] Ibid., 163.

agreed to a cease fire with British commander General Jeremy Moore. The terms of the document signed by both the British and Argentine commanders at the conclusion of combat operations were clear that the capitulation was "not unconditional surrender."[51] British forces won the brief war, assisted by support supported from the commonwealth and NATO.[52] In 100 days of battle the British lost thirty-five aircraft, nine ships sunk or destroyed, thirty-two other vessels sustained varying degrees of damage, 255 personnel were killed in action and 777 wounded. The Argentine Armed Forces lost 117 aircraft, four vessels sunk, four vessels damaged, 635 personnel killed in action, and 1068 wounded.[53] Argentine military forces commenced withdrawing from the Malvinas on June 14, 1982, and the British administration was once again reestablished, but the dispute over the true sovereignty of the islands remains alive.

The facts showed that the War of 1982 was a product of misunderstandings and protracted behaviors to solve the conflict. The real issue is about natural resources control and exploitations. In the 1990 decade relations between Argentina and Great Britain improved. Both countries signed an Agreement of Joint Cooperation Declaration on Off Shore Oil and Gas Exploration around the Malvinas Area. In 2007 the Argentine government voided the Oil and Gas 1995 Exploration declaration because of Great Britain's unilateral actions to exploit the natural resources, reticence to dialogue and will to solve the dispute about Sovereignty.[54]

---

[51] Argentine Army. *Informe Oficial del Ejercito Argentino Tomo II -Conflicto Malvinas* (Buenos Aires-Argentina: Estado Mayor General del Ejercito Argentino 1983): Annex 79.

[52] Stephen Badsey, Rob Havers, and Mark Grove. "*The Falklands Conflict Twenty Years On, Lessons for the Future*": Admiral Sir John Woodward: A personal view. (Frank Cass London New York, 2005), 177.

[53] Ruben Moro, History of the South Atlantic Conflict: The War for the Malvinas (New York-Praeger-London, 1989), 323-332.

[54] http://www.guardian.co.uk/world/2007/mar/28/argentina.oil accessed 4/12/2010.

Section 3: The British perspective

The isolation of the Falklands Islands did not continue,
And in due course the islands were again brought forward
To preoccupy the minds of governments, diplomats and
Navy officers of the three nations which formed the
"South Atlantic Triangle": Argentina, United States and Great Britain".[55]

To address the question of the difference of perspectives it is important to discuss both the British and Argentinean viewpoints. In this section the British worldview will be examined.

The British narrative centers on the theme that the Falklands have been always a British territory, including prior to 1833, and that Argentina has unsuccessfully tried to exercise sovereignty on several occasions. One hundred and forty nine years after the 1833 British occupation, led by an un-democratic military junta, Argentina invaded British territory in 1982. Edmund Yorke argues in his chapter about the Argentine invasion that the Commonwealth was not slow to respond to the crisis in 1982. Commonwealth Secretary-General Sir Shridath Ramphal concluded: *"Argentina did not invade the Falklands to liberate the people of the Islands from the British rule, but to impose Argentine rule over them against their will."*[56]

The geopolitical importance of the Islands has historically been as the "key to the Pacific and Antarctica." While modern technology has somewhat reduced this factor, the prospect of exploiting the islands natural resources in the future has made the islands retain their importance. In their book, *The Battle for the Falklands,* Max Hastings and Simon Jenkins refer to the Malvinas as "The Forgotten Islands" and as the "last war of colonialism" fought by Great Britain.[57] The British position on the

---

[55] Barry Gough, *The Falkland Islands/Malvinas The contest for Empire in the South Atlantic* (The Athlone Press-London and AtlanticHighlands, NJ, 1992), 50.

[56] Shridat Ramphal, *Not Britain's Cause Alone: Address to the Commonwealth Press Union, 15 June, 1982* (London: Commonwealth Secretariat Library, Marlborough House, 1982).

[57] Max Hastings and Simon Jenkins. *The Battle for the Falklands.* (New York: W.W. Norton and Company, 1983), 6 and 12: Chapter I "The Forgotten Islands. The Falklands were never of any great strategic importance – certainly not before the advent of coal-powered vessels. Two of the British possessions: Gibraltar and

Falklands, Georgias and South Sandwich Islands comes from the time of Alfred Thayer Mahan's theories, at the apogee of the British Empire, where the importance of sea power was paramount. Great Britain believes that it owned the Islands before 1833, and that the people living on the islands for more than 150 years have the right of self-determination, and it does not need to engage in dialogue about the issue of sovereignty with Argentina. This is despite the fact that a United Nations resolution recognizes the issue and the need for a diplomatic solution.[58]

The Islands' importance from the British view remains primarily about exploitation of natural resources like oil and controlling key points in the South Atlantic. The Royal Navy used the Islands as a base in World War I and II for operations against the German Navy. As the technology exists today to monitor the world from the space, and Britain's Royal Navy is but a shadow of its former self, this position is tenuous. Britain still sees the islands as a physical base, but in the future the priority will be for economic, not military reasons. The islands reported abundance of natural resources, including commercial fishing grounds, oil & gas,[59] and tourism potential, make them an attractive possession.[60] As previously discussed, the Islands are also well positioned to support activities in Antarctica and the pass to the South Pacific.[61]

The Falklands fell into a special category. They were occupied by people of British background and citizenship but were also claimed by their adjacent foreign state, unlike other cases in which the colonies were proud to be British and there were no dispute."

[58] United Nations Resolution 2065 from the year 1965 that requested the two countries, Argentina and United Kingdom, to negotiate the issue of sovereignty.

[59] Owen Bowcot, *United Kingdom stakes claim to huge area of South Atlantic seabed,* (http//www.guardian.co.uk/world/2009/may/11/uk-falklands-argentina-un accessed 10 Aug 2009): British journal "The Guardian" from 11 May 2009 refers about the issue that: " United Kingdom claimed to a huge area of South Atlantic seabed, United Nation submission heralds battle with Argentina over mineral rights".

[60] Ibid.

[61] Robert Booth, *Falkland Islanders say Argentina is waging economic warfare* (http://www.guardian.co.uk/uk/2009/jun/14/falklands-islands-argentina-economy-industry accessed: 10 Aug 2009): British journal "The Guardian" from 14 June 2009 refers about the idea that Argentina is waging economic warfare.

British Diplomacy - British Rights and Legitimacy over the Islands

Great Britain defends its diplomatic position about rights and legitimacy over the islands with an argument based on self-determination and effective occupation. Argentina did not exercise effective sovereignty over the Falklands and the people that live there wants to be British. Diplomatic misunderstandings over the Falklands/Malvinas between Argentina and Great Britain, particularly over these points, have been constant.

The political environments in both Great Britain and Argentina in 1982 were unstable, making the deteriorating situation even more complex. Many of Prime Minister Margaret Thatcher's economic reform policies instituted in 1980 and 1981 were proving unpopular and ineffective. Relative British military power was weakening due to shrinking budgets. But despite this events occurred, Margaret Thatcher never tempted to compromise the security of British forces for financial reasons.[62]

According to Admiral Sir John Woodward, on March 18-19, 1982, Argentine scrap-metal workers landed at Leith Harbour, South Georgia, and raised the Argentine flag. On April 2, 1982, the Argentine military conducted Operation *Virgin del Rosario* and invaded the Falklands. Argentine Marines landed at Grytviken, South Georgia and the United Nations Security Council adopted Resolution 502 qualifying Argentina as the aggressor. Lord Carrington was removed as foreign secretary and was replaced by Francis Pym.[63]

Argentina made the decision to recover the Islands through military force and humiliate Britain in the action of April 2, 1982. Prime Minister Thatcher issued a strategic communication message by directing the Royal Navy to sail to the South Atlantic. The strategic message was that the British power was alive and well, even though the Royal Navy was in decline.[64]

---

[62] Margaret Thatcher, *The Downing Street Years*, (London: Harper Collins, 1993), 188.

[63] Stephen Badsey, Rob Havers, and Mark Grove. "*The Falklands Conflict Twenty Years On, Lessons for the Future*": Admiral Sir John Woodward: A personal view. (Frank Cass London New York, 2005), 4-5.

[64] Sandy, Woodward, *One Hundred Days: The Memoirs of the Falklands Battle Group Commander*. (Annapolis: Naval Institute Press, 1997), 81-82.

British Admiral Sir Sandy Woodward's operational challenges included how he would approach the Argentine military forces and in which part of the Falklands he would launch his attack. His problems included time, where to land British forces, the Argentine Air Force and naval aviation threats, and his own extended lines of communications.[65] He also wondered if the British warrior ethos was still alive and what role other superpowers would play. On April 25, 1982, things became clearer when British forces recovered Georgias Island and realized that Argentine Forces were not providing strong resistance. The Argentine forces were not there to provide a static defense of the Island; they were just there to protect the Argentine workers.

At the operational level, this war demonstrated that submarines continue to be an important threat in conventional wars. The Royal Navy made great effort to capture the ARA *Santa Fe*, but was unable to destroy Argentina's single remaining German-built conventional submarine ARA *San Luis*, which provided a constant threat to the British task force.[66] The Argentine military provided a brave resistance with an army of conscripts, which lacked sufficient resources and had little training. In land operations at the tactical level, the human factor of the British professional soldier was a key for success.[67]

Finally, the same British narrative addressed the Malvinas military campaign as *"No Picnic"*.[68] The image of a South American country challenging the British military was not conceivable. In the Malvinas War, the Argentine military with an army of conscripts made the professional British military suffer the most significant losses in material since World War II.[69]

---

[65] Ibid.,77-78.

[66] Bruce Watson, and Dunn Peter, *Military Lessons of the Falkland Island War, Views from the United States* (Arms and Armor Press, London-England, 1984), 128.

[67] Ibid., 131.

[68] Jullien, Thompson, *No Picnic*, (London, Butler and Tanner, 1984).

[69] Ruben Moro, History of the South Atlantic Conflict: The War for the Malvinas (New York-Praeger-London, 1989), 342.

British Self- Determination

From the British point of view, the Falklands conflict is not a problem of colonialism, but a problem of self-determination. Francis Toase argues that before April 1, 1982, the United Nations recommended that both countries should negotiate to solve the issue. The General Assembly endorsed Argentina's contention that the removal of British rule from Malvinas was in keeping with the spirit of decolonization. But this United Nations statement neglects the Islanders' right of self-determination. The United Nations called for peaceful negotiations, so if Argentina chose to interpret these resolutions as justifying the use of forces, then this was Argentina's miscalculation and not the United Nation's fault.[70]

Great Britain's experience in managing war and diplomacy overwhelmed Argentine colonial claims. Edmund Yorke states that Suez and Rhodesia had been "a close run thing" for the credibility, and the survival of the Commonwealth.[71] The Malvinas crisis in 1982 engendered fears caused by previous colonial experiences. During the 7 April Commons, Denis Healey asserted: *"the argument in Suez was about property rights; in the Falklands it is about human rights. At Suez the British violated the United Nations Charter. In the Falklands crisis the Argentines have violated the United Nations Charter…Suez offers no precedent here".*[72]

Barry Gough provides valuable insight into the understanding of the British Colonial Office:

"…thus one promoter might call for a "little Gibraltar of the South", another might propose a secure base for Her Majesty ships, and another might foster the idea of a British refuge for British merchantmen. Together, these views added to points of view the Ministry was obliged to consider. The combined weight of argument was in favor of extending British obligations. The British were led to reassert the authority in Falklands Islands by reoccupation in 1832 and 1833 for two reasons: the pressure of rival powers, Argentina and United States, and the threat that the control of the Falklands might have in foreign hands to British seaborne and political interests in South America and Southern Oceans. On 8 December 1914, after the Battle of Falkland Islands against the German Imperial Navy, England held undisputed control of the

---

[70] Stephen Badsey, Rob Havers, and Mark Grove. *"The Falklands Conflict Twenty Years On, Lessons for the Future"*: Admiral Sir John Woodward: A personal view. (Frank Cass London New York, 2005), 162.

[71] Ibid., 176-178.

[72] Ibid., 177-178.

ocean trade routes of the world. The utility of Falklands to Britannia's rule was demonstrated...[73]

The British control of the Falklands spans three centuries and may well enter a fourth. While British interests in Canada, Australia, South Africa, and elsewhere have moved through what has been assumed to be a logical progression in the rise and fall of empires, in the Malvinas the interest has been constant. It defies the usual rules of the British imperial ethos. "Easily acquired, it may yet be the most difficult to dispose of..."[74]

The efforts that Great Britain made to maintain and fund the survival of the small population in the islands since 1833, is not a minor thing. Taking into account the challenges that faced the British since their reoccupation in 1833, through the time of Ernest Shackleton and his expeditions to Antarctica in the beginnings of 1900 decade, the war efforts with Argentina in 1982, all these set the conditions in Great Britain's behavior to disregard the Argentina claims of sovereignty.

In 2007, the Argentine attitude to end the accord "Declaration of Cooperation in Oil Exploration between Argentina and Great Britain" signed in 1995 triggered an escalation in the tensions with Argentina. This distance produced more tensions than agreements. The British Crown issued a Constitution for the Falkland; in 2009 the Islands became part of the "European Union Overseas Territories" ending in the unilateral British explorations that started in February 2010.

In conclusion, the British argument rests on three precedents. Firstly, they discovered (right of discovery) the Islands, asserting a claim in 1765 and never renouncing it. Secondly, the effective occupation of the Islands by Great Britain is a fact. Finally the principle of "self-determination" justifies their occupation of the islands since the majority of the population passionately wants to remain British citizens.[75]

---

[73] Barry Gough, *The Falkland Islands/Malvinas The contest for Empire in the South Atlantic* (The Athlone Press-London and AtlanticHighlands, NJ, 1992), 67, 132, 133.

[74] Ibid., 158-159.

[75] Max Hastings and Simon Jenkins. *The Battle for the Falklands.* (New York-London: WW Norton and Company, 1983), 7-9.

Section 4: The Argentine perspective

> *"The Argentine nation ratifies its legitimate and non-prescribing sovereignty over the Malvinas, Georgias and South Sandwich Islands and over the corresponding maritime and insular zones, as they are an integral part of the national territory. The recovery of said territories and the full exercise of sovereignty, respectful of the way of life of their inhabitants and according to the principles of international law, are a permanent and unrelinquished goal of the Argentine people."*[76]

From analysis of the British perspective, the main factors that differ from the Argentine view were: sovereignty, diplomacy, and colonialism. This section will address the Argentine perspective.

Sovereignty

For Argentina, the transition from Spanish colony to nationhood transpired due to a decline in Spanish power and strategic reach. The 1808 French invasion severely taxed Spain's ability to effectively manage their colonies. The vacuum created by the lack of Spanish strategic reach was seen as an opportunity by Britain, who looked to secure the undefended Spanish possessions for their empire. In Argentina's case, the British efforts to conquer and colonize Argentina were unsuccessful. These events feature prominently in the Argentine narrative of the Malvinas history. The nineteenth century environment was very specific regarding international boundaries and the new states that were created following the decline of Spain and the rise of Great Britain. Between the eighteenth and twentieth century's, important political and international changes occurred that included boundary shifts and political revolutions throughout the Americas. While political anarchy still exists in some parts of the

---

[76] *Argentine National Constitution- Temporary Provisions-* First Article. The last reform that had the Argentine Constitution was in 1994. During the reform, it was concluded that Argentina will not use the military force again with the case of Malvinas, but that the diplomatic claim will not be over. In those days, the relations between Argentina and Great Britain were the best after the war of 1982. This provision in the Constitution had been put in the text during the presidency of Carlos Menem who governed Argentina since 1990 for two consecutive periods until 1998.

world, the majority is politically stable and has evolved through a combination of war, respect, and tolerance; and has primarily been conducted among western nations.

The problem of sovereignty has generated most of the misunderstanding, such as the occupation of the Malvinas by the Argentine military in April 1982, and the British sinking of the Argentine Cruiser *General Belgrano,* which escalated the conflict. The British decision to use their veto power as a permanent member of the United Nations Security Council, against a country that is not, made the situation more complex. Additionally, Argentina had to consider the possibility of the use of nuclear weapons by Britain, if it was unable to regain the islands through conventional means.[77]

According to the international doctrine of prescription,[78] the British thought that they could legally claim ownership of the Malvinas after 150 years of occupation. Argentina decided to resort to military means in 1982, after *149 years* of British occupation making the doctrine of prescription useless.

Unfortunately, Argentina and Great Britain have failed to solve the sovereignty issues and the colonialism concerns regarding the Malvinas. According to different official sources in Argentina, the reasons why Argentina continues to claim the Islands are because Malvinas, Georgias and South Sandwich were considered a disputed area by United Nations Resolution 2065, which gave them a particular status.[79] The self-determination argument did not apply in Malvinas case because the population is not native but inserted.[80] Argentina, on the other hand, has claimed persistently for over 149 years that the population in Malvinas is not a colonized native population.[81]

---

[77] Rob Evans and Leigh David, "Falklands Warships Carried Nuclear Weapons, Ministry of Defense admits." http:// www.guardian.co.uk/politics/2003/dec06/military.freedomofinformation/ accessed 10/25/2009.

[78] The International doctrine of prescription is an international legal term and means that if you occupy a territory for 150 years without any claim, then you own it forever. It is not applicable anymore in the Malvinas case because Argentina cut the continuous British occupation in 1982 (From 1833 to 1982 passed 149 years), claimed its own rights and sovereignty over the islands since 1833 and still continues doing it.

[79] United Nations Resolution 2065 of 1965 that requested the two countries to negotiate the issue of sovereignty.

[80] United Nations Resolution 2353 (1968): For a similar case in Gibraltar, clearly expressed that self-determination could not be applied when the colonial situation affected territorial integrity and national unity.

[81] The Malvinas currently has a population of 2478 inhabitants, born in Great Britain or in the Malvinas.

For Argentina, the Malvinas are Argentine. Of course for Great Britain it is the opposite. The current issues and ill-feeling between the nations would not exist if the problem had been addressed earlier, just after the British occupation of the Malvinas in 1833, by a subsequent treaty or sale of the islands (as per the case of Alaska for the United States). In any case, both actors should recognize that the Malvinas Islands might be or British or Argentinean. Recognition from both countries on the scope of the problem would shape in other ways the attitudes and behaviors in future negotiations between Argentina and Great Britain. Reality shows us that that is not the case, because of a lack of effective communication and protracted diplomacy executed by the United Nations. Both Argentina and Great Britain have failed to act in accordance with United Nations resolutions.

It is important to recognize that the current control of the Malvinas is not the same as it was in 1833, or even as it was in 1982. Physical control is not the problem – a lesson learned by Argentina in 1982. The issue is about sovereignty of states and avoiding colonialist-like behaviors.

Diplomacy

The causes of the 1982 had been diplomatic misunderstandings and overreactions from both, the Argentine and British governments. The Georgias Islands incident, regarding the status of Argentine civilian workers, occurred due to a lack of effective communication.[82] This event and others were clearly the consequences of Great Britain neglecting to discuss the issue of sovereignty with Argentina, despite the United Nations recommendations.[83] The key impediment to negotiations from the Argentine perspective is the lack of effective communications from both sides and the reluctance of Great Britain to enter into meaningful dialogue over sovereignty.

---

[82] Sergio Fernandez, *Malvinas 1982: Symmetrical Misunderstandings and overreactions lead the way to war*, (United States Army War College, 2002), 38. The incident in the Georgias Islands, with the British military that arresting Argentine civilian workers, was one of the key events that drove to the decision to launch the Argentine Military Operation *Virgin del Rosario* to protect the workers and recover the Malvinas for Argentina.

[83] United Nations Resolution 2065 of 1965 that requested the two countries negotiate the sovereignty issue.

The perception in Argentina goes beyond physical boundaries and embraces legitimacy, integral territoriality, history, culture, right of self-determination and the ethical connotation of freedom that exists across South America. MERCOSUR (South Economic Market) and UNASUR (Union of South American Nations) are two examples of South American cooperation that display the strong bonds that unite new democracies forging ahead in a post-colonial world. For Argentina, the Malvinas continues to be a protracted conflict about sovereignty and colonialism. The war of 1982 did not change anything from the Argentine perspective. If the goal of war is to achieve a long-term or a stable peace, this conflict did not do so as Argentina sees the continuing of British occupation as illegitimate.

The Argentine view also raises the argument of self-determination, but for Argentina it is the right of self-determination for the entire Argentine population (more than forty million today) in a post-colonial age. Argentina also views a continuing British occupation as colonial intent that violates the geographic integrity of the Argentine country.

The misunderstandings that caused the war over the Malvinas continued even during the conflict, as it was waged by two militaries that felt more allies than enemies. The British narrative focuses on military victory, rather war termination criteria and or an end state. It does not address the Argentine perception that this war did not solve anything.

Argentina went to war unprepared. Strategically, the Malvinas War was a failure for Argentina, because the strategy did not adequately address the connection between means, ways, and clear end state; a critical requirement in the decision-making process. Although the military strategy failed, the claim was and remains legitimate in the Argentine and South American perception.

The War for Malvinas from the Argentine perspective consisted of two main campaigns conducted in five phases. The first campaign, the recovery, took place from 25 March until 7 April 1982. The second campaign, the defense, was fought from 7 April until June 14, 1982. Following the recovery campaign, Argentina established a Military Governor in Port Argentino, General Mario Benjamin Menendez. The Argentinean Phase III, dominate, and Phase IV stability were easily achieved as there was not a single British military or civilian casualty. Phase V, enabling civil authority, took place with the transition from the British Governor to the Argentine one.

The Argentine Recovery Campaign: Operation Virgin del Rosario

Argentina's broad strategic intent was to occupy the Malvinas, Georgias and South Sandwich to protect Argentinean workers in Georgias Island and to improve Argentina's position for future negotiations with Britain over sovereignty. This was accomplished during Operation *Virgin del Rosario* on April 2, 1982, when an Argentine Amphibian Task Force landed in Puerto Argentino (Port Stanley) without loss of British life. Argentina executed the operation very rapidly, with planning, training and preparation for the operation only beginning on March 23, 1982.

On March 25, 1982, the Argentine government decided to conduct military operations to recover the Malvinas Islands. The Argentinean National Strategy Directive 1/82 (DENAC 1/82)[84] did not describe a desired end state. In this DENAC, there was no description of a timeline for the operation, because it was to be conditional on the progress of diplomatic negotiations. It was DENAC 2/82,[85] issued to compliment DENAC 1/82, that detailed further actions to consolidate the political objective to restore the sovereignty over Malvinas, Georgias and South Sandwich Islands. Based on DENAC 2/82, Argentina's Military Strategy Directive 1/82 (DEMIL 1/82) read: "the employment of part of the Argentine military power to seize, consolidate, and achieve the strategic military objective in the most favorable of circumstances, congruent with the previous resolution from the Military Committee."[86]

As the campaign plan was developed rapidly, there was no accurate joint intelligence preparation of the battlefield for this war. Schematic Recovery and Defense Campaign Plans were developed directly

---

[84] Argentine Army. *Informe Oficial del Ejercito Argentino Tomo I -Conflicto Malvinas.* Buenos Aires-Argentina: Estado Mayor General del Ejercito Argentino 1983.DENAC 1/82 (Argentine National Strategic Directive= Directiva Estrategica Nacional nro 01/82), 21.

[85] Ibíd. DENAC 2/82 (Argentine National Strategic Directive = Directiva Estrategica Nacional nro 02/82, April 1982), 21.

[86] Ibid. DEMIL 1/82 (National Military Strategy Directive = Directiva Estrategica Militar nro 1/82, April 1982), 21: the stated mission was: "employ part of the Argentine military power to occupy and maintain the Malvinas, Georgias, and South Sandwich Islands."

from the Argentine National Military Strategy, but there was not an overall concept of operations for the Malvinas, as this war surprised not only the British but also many in the Argentinean government and military.

The original plan to recover the Malvinas Islands was based on the intent to seize the capital of Malvinas, Port Argentine (Port Stanley), with a small Argentine military force, without British or civilian casualties. Once secured, then the British and Argentina could negotiate the sovereignty of the Malvinas through diplomatic processes, with Argentina holding a stronger bargaining position than before. The entire military operation was not expected to last more than five days.[87]

Operation *Virgin del Rosario* began on the morning of April 2, 1982, by a small joint force consisting of personnel from the Argentine Army IX Brigade, and an Argentine naval force that contributed ships and commando troops. The Argentine Air Force consolidated the Argentinean position by air-landing troops after the seizure of Port Argentino airfield. Port Argentino was secured at 1230 on April 2, 1982. Operation *Virgin del Rosario* was an example of tactical and operational professionalism. It was a tactical surprise that accomplished the mission without inflicting casualties. Argentinean troops respected the civilian populace, which at the time of the war numbered approximately 1800 inhabitants. Captured British military personnel were handled according to the Geneva Convention of 1949 at all times.

The Argentine Defense Campaign

After recovering the Islands on April 2, 1982, there was no Argentine sequel to stay and fight a defensive battle. Everything that followed was improvised. The vital assumptions made unilaterally by the military junta included that Great Britain lacked the strategic reach and political will to fight to recover the islands, and that the United States would remain neutral. There was no contingency branch

---

[87] Argentine Army. *Informe Oficial del Ejercito Argentino Tomo I -Conflicto Malvinas.* Buenos Aires-Argentina: Estado Mayor General del Ejercito Argentino 1983), 27-29. Operation *Virgin del Rosario* was the only plan to recover the Islands.

plans or sequels developed. On April 4, 1982, the United States authorized Great Britain to use Ascension Island as an intermediate staging base. This development dramatically changed the situation for Argentina because it now put British forces only 3000 nautical miles from the Islands.[88]

Argentina's lack of understanding and inaccurate appreciation of intelligence led to this critical error. The Argentine intelligence assessment stated that Argentina would be unable to hold the islands if Great Britain was supported by United States in a recovery campaign. The error was that Argentina assumed away the possibility of American support for their staunch allies, the British. United Nations Resolution 502 condemned the Argentine military action as an aggression and the British Royal Navy commenced preparations to sail to the South Atlantic with a large task force as it could muster.[89]

On April 7, 1982, Britain declared a maritime exclusion zone of 200 nautical miles around the Malvinas, to come into effect from 0400 hours April 12. United Nations' diplomacy was blocked by Great Britain, who held veto power as a permanent member of the Security Council.

The decision to sink the *Belgrano* was triggered by the Argentine military occupation of the Malvinas, but the choice to escalate the dispute into war was questionable considering that up to that point there were no British casualties in the conflict.

The attack on the British aircraft carrier *Invincible* is a point of contention between the narratives, but exists as a critical part of the Argentine view. On May 29 1982, the Argentine Air Force launched an attack against the HMS Carrier *Invincible* in order to try to achieve the strategic effect of crippling Britain's air superiority of the Islands in one stroke. Two Super Etendard jets from the Argentine Navy, armed with Argentina's last Exocet A/S 39 anti-ship missiles, and four Argentine Air Force A-4C attack aircraft, armed with 500-pound bombs were tasked to accomplish this mission. The approach was accomplished with two air-to-air refueling sorties south of the Malvinas. According to Argentina and

---

[88] Bruce Watson and Peter Dunn, *Military lessons of the Falkland Island War, views from the United States* (Arms and Armor Press, London-England, 1984), 148-149.

[89] Stephen Badsey, Rob Havers and Mark Grove, *The Falklands Conflict Twenty Years On, Lessons for the Future*: The United Nations Security Resolution 502 by Francis Toase (Frank Cass, London –New York, 2005), 161.

unofficial British sources, the Exocet and three 500-pound bombs impacted on the *Invincible*. Britain has never officially acknowledged any damage to the *Invincible* in this attack. British air defense Sea Dart missiles shot down two Argentine aircraft during the air attack, but according to Argentina, the mission was accomplished. By June 14 1982, the Argentine Army Aviation was still flying under British air local superiority and bad weather conditions trying to support the last defenses in Port Argentine. The Argentine artillery fired all the ammunition available in the Islands. Even if the Argentine Armed Forces had been more effective in battle or had more resources with which to fight, the British military victory would have only been delayed. Nothing would have changed the military outcome of the Malvinas war.

The main military lessons learned from the Argentine perspective was that in any future conventional war, the operations in theater have to be designed with regard to joint and interagency concepts, and forces must be able to provide mutual support. Around the time of the Malvinas War, the United States was creating their School of Advanced Military Studies. Its creation in some ways was a result of the gaps discovered in the Joint and Army doctrine displayed in the Malvinas; one of them was the doctrine of the Air Land Operations. These lessons were added to others from the Israeli campaigns of Yom Kippur in 1973 and the Bekaa Valley in 1982. Other lessons learned from the failures in joint operations in Malvinas were reflected years later in the Goldwater- Nichols Act of 1986. The successful Argentine air and submarine operations against the Royal Navy provided excellent tactical effects, but no operational success. This was because the actions of the Argentine Air Force and naval aviation, Navy surface and subsurface operations, and Argentine Army operations, were not synchronized to support land maneuver on the Islands.

The events that took place in this particular environment framed and shaped the international behavior of these countries. Now is the time to look at things differently and ask different questions, as this situation still adversely affects important relations between Great Britain and Argentina. Meta - questions such as why Argentina and Great Britain cannot reassume a dialogue over sovereignty when they were so close to doing so immediately prior to the war; how we understand colonialist-like behavior in the 21st century; and which will be the role of the United Nations if countries are selective about which resolutions they choose to obey.[90]

In 1995 there was a cooperation accord about Oil Exploration signed by both countries and the Argentine President Carlos Saul Menem visited Great Britain for the first time after the war. In 2007, the Argentine president Nestor Kirchner withdrew from that Accord due to the lack of transparency and unilateral decisions made by Great Britain in Oil explorations. The British response was the new Falkland Islands Constitution, implemented in January 2009, which exacerbates the conflict making the problem more complex.[91] It demonstrates that the British no longer look to a negotiated settlement. In Argentina this unilateral action made by Great Britain was perceived as a step towards independence of an hypothetical island country of less than 2600 inserted British people, in a territory that still is in dispute. A positive step took place in October 2009, when Argentine relatives of the soldiers killed in combat in 1982 were authorized by the British government to fly and visit the Argentine cemetery in Darwin-Goose Green.[92] In November 2009, the European Union's Lisbon Declaration stated that the Falklands are part of the European domain, disregarding the fact that they are a territory in dispute according to the United Nations. Argentina has protested to all the European countries that signed the declaration.[93] By November 2009, the Argentine president delivered the National Defense Policy in which she stressed Argentine sovereignty over the Malvinas as a national interest.[94]

---

[90] United Nations resolution 502: The use of the right of veto by United Kingdom during the War in 1982 was seen as an embarrassing for the members that do not belong to the Permanent Security Council of United Nations.

[91] *New Falklands Constitution Agreed*, http://news.bbc.co.uk/2/hi/uk_news/politics/7713948.stm accessed 10/1/2010.

[92] On October 2009, British Prime Minister Gordon Brown and Argentine President Cristina Fernandez de Kirchner agreed to authorize Argentine relatives to visit the Darwin Argentine Cemetery in the Malvinas on humanitarian grounds.

[93] *Energetic claim to the EU for Malvinas*, http://www.lanacion.com.ar/nota.asp?nota_id=1206308 accessed 10/1/2010.

[94] Cristina Fernandez de Kirchner, Argentine Official National Bulletin 31779: Presidential Decree 1714/2009 Annex I Chapter II: Argentine National Defense Policy (Ministry of Defense, 12 November 2009), 5.

In February 2010, Great Britain started unilateral exploration of oil in the vicinity of the Malvinas, disregarding the United Nations resolution which states that the Islands are still a territory in dispute. This move only serves to increase the virulence of the conflict, and has unpredictable political consequences for both nations.

Argentine popular view

The Argentine civil population today has hundreds of Centers of Veterans from the Malvinas War, and thousand of public monuments with the name *"Malvinas Argentinas."* On April 2, every year Argentina celebrates the *Argentine Veterans of War National Day.*

A necessary condition to satisfy the Argentinean populace is addressing the lack of British transparency. Argentina opened all their files after the war, but Great Britain continues to maintain secrecy, mainly due to the veiled threat of nuclear weapons that the Argentine society perceived the British intended to use in that conflict.[95]

In general terms, the popular Argentine perception is that Argentina and Great Britain, two friendly nations, went to war in 1982 over a dispute regarding the sovereignty of the Malvinas Islands. A concern to Argentina is that the United States supported the United Kingdom against the principles of the Monroe Doctrine and against its long-held principle to end colonialism. There is a great deal of literature that refers to the reasons why both countries went to war. Some attribute the primary causes to the Argentine military junta and Margaret Thatcher's political goal to remain in power. Argentina did not seek support from the Soviets. The Argentine internal war against communism and terrorism in the 1970s had largely been fought by the same Argentine military junta.

Neither the behavior of both countries nor the studies of the potential causes of the War of 1982 can interact favorably with the natural propensity of the environment to achieve desirable end state for Argentina. A decision from a supra-national institution like United Nations or through international

---

[95] Rob Evans and Leigh David, "Falklands Warships Carried Nuclear Weapons, Ministry of Defense admits." http:// www.guardian.co.uk/politics/2003/dec06/military.freedomofinformation/ accessed 10/25/2009.

arbitration is required, in order to contain the uncertainty of the Argentine population. The "Malvinization effect" in Argentina can be used to create a potential environment in Argentina that has only two possibilities: going closer to or further away from western values and interests of United States and Great Britain. This effect is felt beyond the borders of Argentina in wider South America.

The nature of the problem leads to the deduction that the areas of intervention are political, diplomatic and economic. The first step in transforming from the observed system to the desired is enabling a culture of engagement between Great Britain and Argentina, in order to build trust, credibility and transparency. This may result in South America becoming more isolated from Great Britain, and by proxy also harm South American relations with the United States. The worst case sees right or left-wing extremists toppling an Argentinean government seen to be weak in the face of colonialism. This could become a base grievance for the rise of an insurgency that would be sure to spread beyond the borders of Argentina.

The military is just only one of the tools that governments have to be able to address the complexity of the international environment. There is no one solution to complex problems like the sovereignty of the Malvinas Islands. A recommended approach to develop a solution strategy to the Malvinas conflict could be to focus more on commonalities between Argentina and Great Britain than differences between them.

The United Nations is arguably the most important creation to come out of the carnage of World War II. The commencement of a dialogue between the belligerents is a key factor in developing any solution to the Malvinas issue. The United Nations must have the power to enforce such a dialogue. The ability of one side to unilaterally refuse to engage due to its power as a permanent member of the Security Council is flawed. If United Nations continues to be unable to affect an issue such as the Malvinas, it will continue to lose respect and legitimacy throughout the world.

Once dialogue has commenced, Argentina and Great Britain should move forward and develop a culture of engagement through constructive discourse to try and craft a solution to end the dispute.

Argentina should engage in discussions with the inhabitants of the islands and the people of Great Britain. Great Britain should clearly explain their position about sovereignty of the Islands to the government and Argentina's people. Feedback generated from this outreach will assist in providing pathways towards walking together to a possible solution. It will certainly take time, but the most important factor for both parties is to focus on the future rather than the past. It is also important to look at the whole system, not just at the relationship between Argentina and Great Britain. Today the Malvinas problem touches actors in the European Union, South America, and the United States. Argentina and Great Britain have to learn and adapt to each other in order to work together.

Today, using the concept of design, it is possible to enhance our understanding of the environment to reframe the problem, in order to develop possible solutions which could enhance the relationships between Great Britain, the United States, and Argentina. Unfortunately, Great Britain and the United States have repeatedly displayed recalcitrant behavior in regard to negotiating a solution to the Malvinas issue.

The legal Perspective: Malvinas in the Argentine National Constitution

The Argentine Constitution was re-written in 1994, and identified the Malvinas dispute as state policy, independent from the policy of whatever government is administrating the country. This has cemented the Malvinas issue firmly into the Argentine cultural narrative, and it will prevail until this issue is solved. United Nations' resolutions provide the groundwork to recommence dialogue between Great Britain and Argentina.

The Argentine constitution states: "The Argentine Nation ratifies its legitimate and non-prescribing sovereignty over the Malvinas, Georgias and South Sandwich Islands and over the corresponding maritime and insular zones, as they are an integral part of the national territory. The recovery of said territories and the full exercise of sovereignty, respectful of the way of life of their inhabitants and according to the principles of international law, are a permanent and unrelinquished goal of the Argentine people."[96] This article perpetuates the issue across Argentinean generations, and will continue to influence Argentine and Anglo-American relations.

Colonialism

The British narrative of the independence process in South America does not reflect the South American viewpoint. Simon Bolivar was not the only *George Washington* in South America. General *San Martin* is Argentina's most famous Argentine national hero. San Martin led the "Argentine Liberty Campaign," crossing the Andes with the Argentine Army, and fighting and winning the battles of Chacabuco and Maipo in Chile. Moreover, he supported Chile and Peru's independence movements, which brought freedom from Spain for these countries. Additionally, he also set the conditions for Ecuador's liberty, defeating the Spanish center of gravity that was in Lima- Peru. He started fighting in the north of Buenos Aires in San Lorenzo in 1812 and ended in Guayaquil-Ecuador by 1820, liberating half South American continent. He rejected all honors and never entered politics in Argentina, later dying in France in almost total poverty. San Martin was an authentic Argentine soldier that fought on behalf of freedom. The end of colonial process was not only occurring in the north of America; it was alive and well in the South too.

Great Britain's empire peaked during the Victorian and the Boer era of the nineteenth century. The British successfully seized Ciudad del Cabo (later Cape Town) in South Africa in 1806, but Buenos Aires repulsed British invasion attempts in 1806 and 1807. However, Great Britain was successful in seizing the Malvinas Islands by force in 1833.[97] Britain also occupied and converted Singapore into a powerful naval base in 1826, and by 1850, India was completely occupied. Other territory conquered by

---

[96] *Argentine National Constitution - Temporary Provisions*- First Article. Argentine undertook constitutional reform in 1994. During the process, Argentina decided not to use military force again to attempt to recover the Malvinas, but only to pursue the issue through diplomatic means. In this period, the relationship between Argentina and Great Britain were recovering after the war of 1982. This provision in the Constitution occurred during the presidency of Carlos Menem, who governed Argentina for two consecutive terms from 1990 until 1998.

[97] Ruben Moro, The History of the South Atlantic Conflict-The War for the Malvinas: The Seeds of War, New York- Praeger 1989), 3.

Great Britain in this period included Australia, Canada, Gibraltar, Suez, New Zealand, and various possessions in the Antilles, Oceania, and in China.[98]

Geographically, Argentina does not seek to build or maintain an empire in the South Atlantic. Argentina considers the Malvinas, Georgias and South Sandwich Islands as a contiguous part of the continental shelf of the Argentine Sea, which has been under its sovereignty since the Spanish colonial period and legitimized by the international precedent of *Uti Possidetis Iure*.[99] The British narrative argues that the inhabitants have lived on the islands for more than 150 years (the period recognized internationally as "prescription," where the inhabitants legally own the territory as nobody else has claimed it), and have the right of self-determination. Great Britain refuses to engage Argentina on the issue of sovereignty although United Nations resolutions demand that such a dialogue exist.[100]

Today, most see the Malvinas dispute as obsolete. The strategic communication message encoded from Great Britain is decoded by the international audience in a negative manner, particularly in South America. It is an antiquated argument, based on colonial geopolitical positions. A potential remedy lies in fostering legitimacy, trust and credibility between Argentina and Great Britain.

Historically, Argentina and Great Britain have maintained good relations much like any other countries in the world. This positive relationship is key in order to address the points of coincidence and agreement instead of focusing on points of disagreement. Despite the fact that Argentina is not a member of the Commonwealth, economically, it has been an open market to all western investment. Argentina understood well the notions of free markets, free trade, and freedom of navigation, and was generally respectful of international standards and behavior. Unfortunately, political instability, a lack of

---

[98] Graciela Corizzo, Conflicts in the South Atlantic: The unfortunate usurpation of Port Deseado (Buenos Aires-Argentina: Circulo Militar, 1988), 27.

[99] *Uti Possidetis Iure* is right to inherit territory from the previously occupying colonial power when a nation gains independence, Examples include Australia's independence from Great Britain, and Argentina's independence from Spain. In Australia's case, all of the islands on the continent's continental shelf (and many others further afield), became Australian sovereign territory upon independence.

[100] United Nations Resolution 2353 (1968): Gibraltar is a similar case. The UN clearly identified that self-determination could not be applied when the colonial situation affected territorial integrity and the national unity.

democratic governance, and corruption did not help to consolidate that behavior. Despite the 1982 war, Argentina is the only South American country that became a major non-NATO ally of the United States in the 1990s.

The enduring result of the war is that the maps of the world bear the inscription: *"Falklands Islands (Malvinas) administered by UK and claimed by Argentina."* Many maps in United Sates and Great Britain though only refer to the territory as: *"Falkland Islands (United Kingdom)."*

This lack of understanding continues to affect international relations, not only between Argentina and Great Britain, but also indirectly for the United States within the South American region. The other crucial aspect that has determined the change in the current environment is the relevance of the flattening of global communications, and how it continues to influence international behavior, which from the Argentinean viewpoint addresses the British presence in Malvinas as colonial behavior.

Section 5: Conclusions

The current control of the Malvinas is not the same as it was in 1833, or even as it was in 1982. Physical control is not the problem – a lesson learned by Argentina in 1982. The issue is about sovereignty of states and avoiding colonialist-like behaviors.

Leaders must understand each side's perspective in order to have a reasonable interpretation of events and frame the right problem. The British and Argentine perspectives differed because their views have been shaped by their respective local narratives. Benedetto Croce expressed this in his famous dictum: "Where there is no narrative, there is no history."[101] The Argentine and the British perspectives differ in terms of divorced narratives and recent events about disputes on Oil Exploitation in 2010, which have permitted the issue to regain momentum, due to the persistent lack of their shared understanding (See Appendix IV).

Only by understanding all perspectives we can address the right discourse and tensions between all the nations involved. In the Malvinas case, four main tensions emerge, which this study of competing narratives aims to synthesize. These tensions are sovereignty, colonialism, self-determination and effective occupation (See Appendix IX).

British perspective

Great Britain's view of the conflict is based on the idea that the Islands are British, they own and effectively occupy the Islands and the problem of sovereignty has been solved. From their view, the War of 1982 was an "Argentine invasion" and intent to usurp the British undisputed sovereignty (See Appendix II).

---

[101] Hayden White, *The Content of the Form- Narrative Discourse and Historical Representation: The Question of Narrative in Contemporary Historical Theory* (John Hopkins University Press, Baltimore, London, 1987), 28.

The strongest British argument rests in the principle of "self-determination," by which the majority of population in the Islands wants to remain British. The problem framed by Great Britain focused in the idea that the only way they will talk about sovereignty with Argentina is when the local people from the Islands want that dialogue. Great Britain has already made great efforts to maintain the Islands and exercised sovereignty without interruptions since 1833. The style of life of the local population in the islands is one of the wealthiest, have its' own Constitution, and the economy envisions a great future with the oil exploration that started in February 2010.

In the British view, the conflict of the Falklands was solved in June of 1982 by a war. The military victory solved the dispute about sovereignty with Argentina.

Argentine Perspective

The assumption that the Falklands conflict is over by an outcome of a military victory, is totally disconnected with the reality that is lived not only in Argentina but also in the entire Latin America. Argentina still has unresolved issues in the Malvinas conflict. In Argentine narratives, the Malvinas Georgias and South Sandwich are part of the South American continental shelf, located in the Argentine sea, a point that from the British view is irrelevant. For Argentina, the War of 1982 was "a recovery to negotiate" and not an invasion, because there cannot be invasion on own territory. In it's eyes, the conflict was based on misunderstanding, colonialism and sovereignty. People believe that their nation inherited the Malvinas through *Uti Possidetis Iure,* and has persistently tried to claim sovereignty. *As Argentina sees its claim as legitimate, it remains persistent.* From it's view, the 2.478 civilians that today continue living in the Islands are not true native people, they are colonists or the descendants of colonists inserted from Great Britain.[102] Although this situation exists, Argentina already addressed the self-determination

---

[102] Government of the Falklands Islands. *The Falklands Island Government: People.* 2009. http://www.falklands.gov.fk//Falklands_Life.html (accessed: 13 August 2009).

aspect in its national constitution with the commitment "...to respect the way of life from the Malvinas, Georgias and South Sandwichs' inhabitants".

The way ahead

The "so what" in comparing the narratives in the Malvinas/ Falklands case, is the output which is a new narrative to gain "shared understanding". The problem framing aspect of the design process tries to address the question: "What are the problems that need to be addressed in the Malvinas issue?" Each side exhibits a system of opposition. For Great Britain, it lies in its reticence to engage in any dialogue about sovereignty over the Malvinas with Argentina. For Argentina, it is its refusal to recognize the issue of self-determination of the inhabitants of the Islands. Both are products of the lack of effective communication between the respective governments.

With both perspectives more clear and the tensions addressed, we can reframe the problem adding to the initial understanding: the "lack of shared meaning and understanding" between the two actors. This issue touches also United States as a strong ally from Great Britain and Argentina. In the current information environment, the tendency to isolate and cut the dialogue between Argentina and Great Britain spreads increasing the virulence of the conflict and generating roots for instability in the Latin American region. Argentina must with diplomacy, directly engage with Great Britain. Great Britain must acknowledge that exist a legitimate Argentine perspective. Moving a step forward to generate the mindset towards a "Change to cooperate" is more an attitude to innovate and harness the complexity of possible solutions in partnership than a technical process to solve the dispute.

The international community must understand that there is a bias associated with the United Nation's resolutions that was evident when Great Britain used its veto power. There was no and still is no; mechanism to compel the nations to engage in a dialogue about sovereignty. There was communication only one way, the British way, and it did not accept the Argentine view. Strategic communications need to be two-way, with feedback addressed, to promote shared meaning and legitimacy (See Appendix VI).

The United States is a key player in the international environment, and the world watch its actions and behaviors. South America understands the "say-do" gap that exists between words and actions, in particular with the implication that the United States will provide support to another country. Solving the Malvinas dispute is more an opportunity than a problem for the United States, where it can act on behalf of legitimacy and generate greater trust from its brothers in South America. The United States and Argentina have faced the same terrorist threats with attacks against their homelands, in Argentina in 1992 and 1994, and in the United States in 1993 and 2001; but instead of fighting together, incidents such as the Malvinas have proven a barrier prohibiting improved relations.

Understanding the values of partnership, legitimacy, and cultural awareness, the approach to the solution cannot be made by one actor alone. Both Argentina and Great Britain share credibility within the international community. They have to provide an example of two mature western countries, which engage in constructive dialogue, and come to an agreement in order to look ahead to the future and walk in the same direction as key global partners. It is imperative that leaders on both sides of this issue understand the different narratives and strive to eliminate the barriers to cooperation.

Appendix I: Argentine Map of the Malvinas Islands

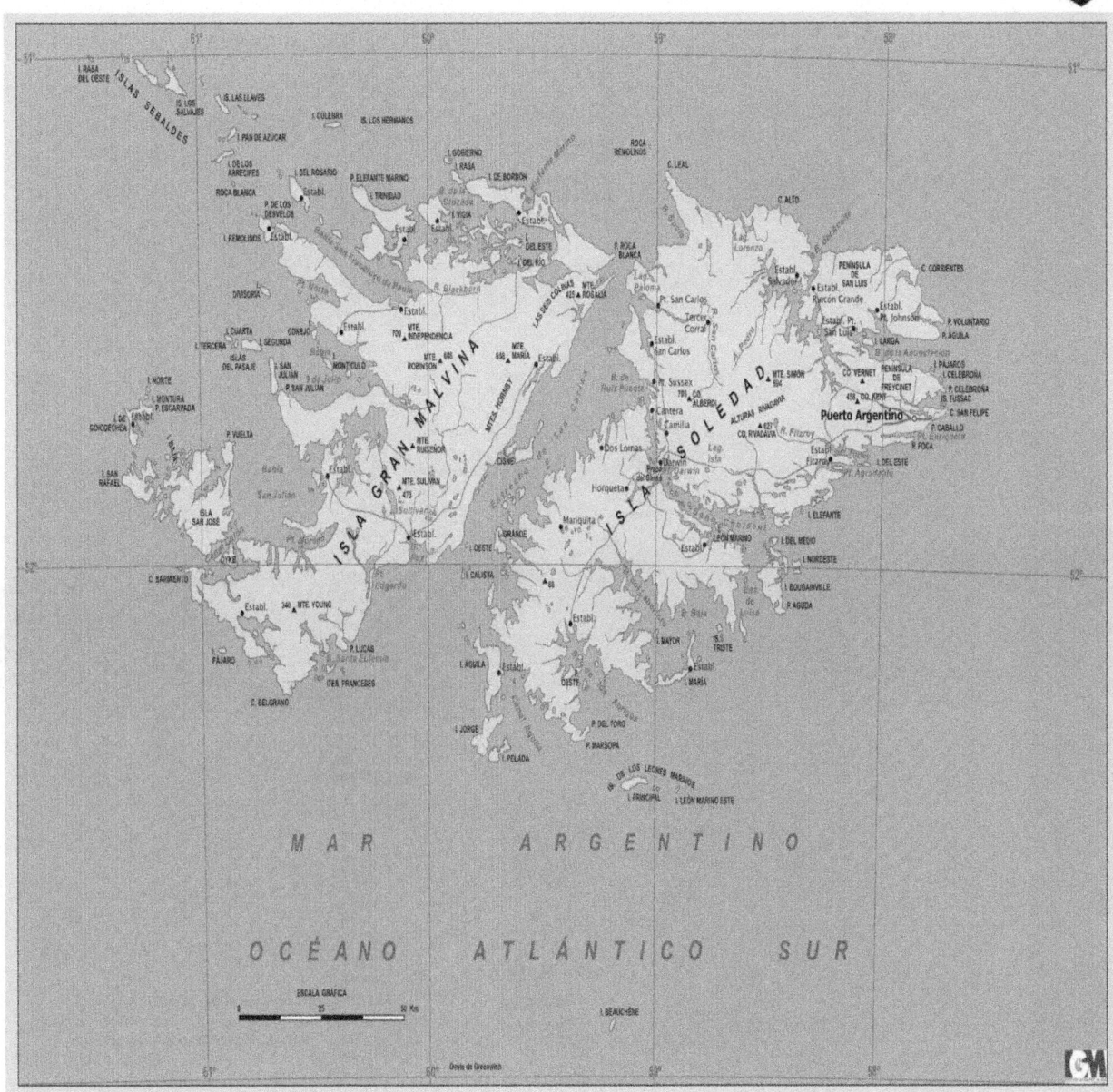

Figure 1: The Malvinas Islands.

Source: http://www.argentina.gov.ar/argentina/portal/documentos/malvinas.pdf accessed 24 Mar 2010

Appendix II: Relative Location of the Malvinas

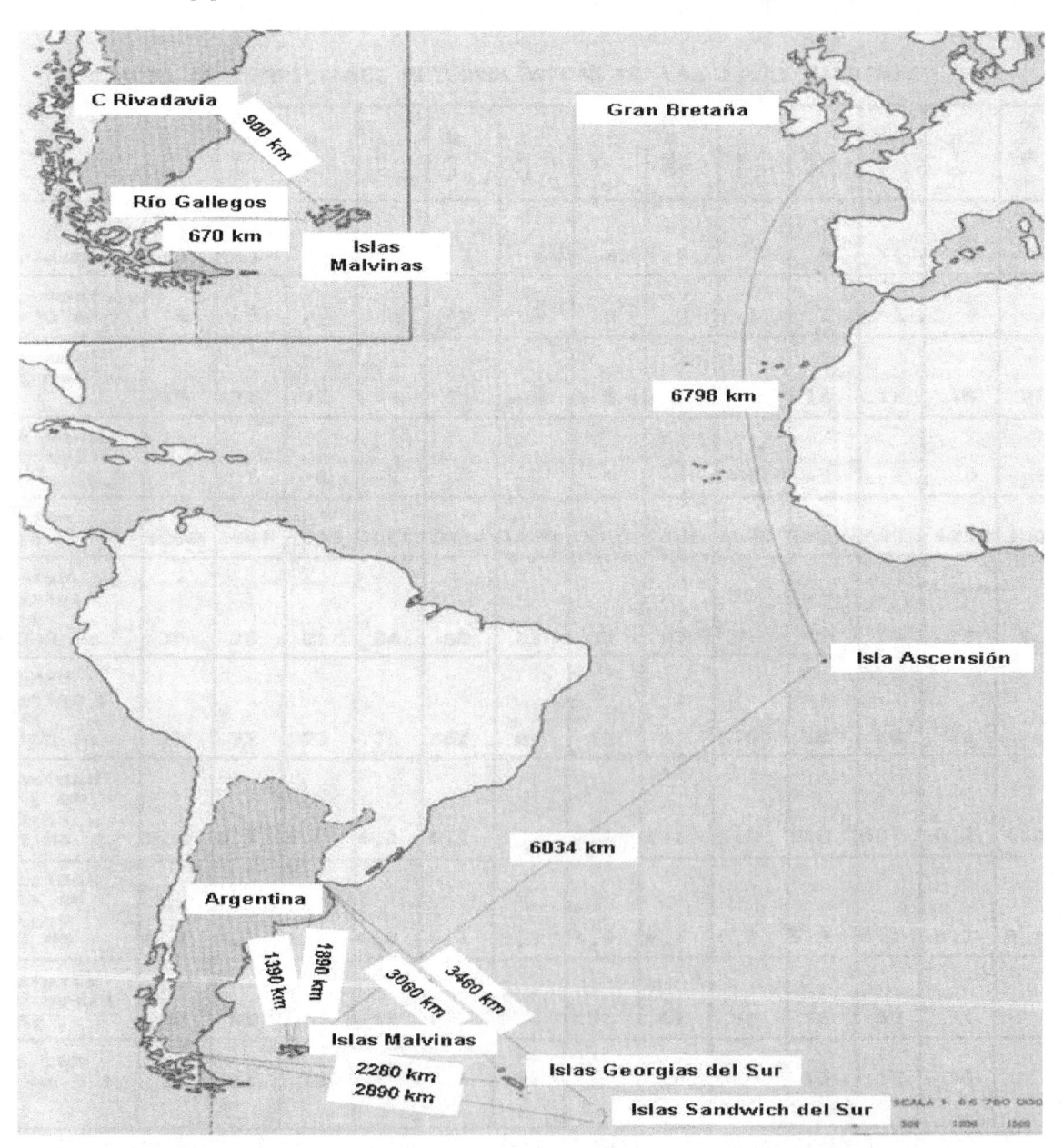

Figure 2: Relative locations of the Malvinas, Georgias and South Sandwich Islands in the South Atlantic Ocean.
Source: Argentine Army. *Informe Oficial del Ejercito Argentino Tomo II -Conflicto Malvinas* (Buenos Aires-Argentina: Estado Mayor General del Ejercito Argentino 1983): Annex 2, Appendix 1.

Appendix III: Surrender Document

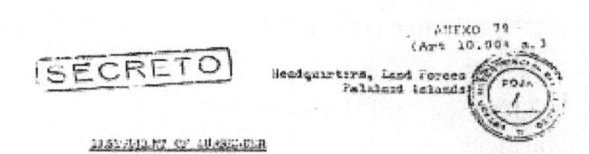

Figure 3: Malvinas War of 1982 document of surrender. This document does not appear normally in British sources, despite the fact is in a London Museum. The word "unconditional" is crossed out with the Argentine Commander's General Mario Benjamin Menendez's initials.

Source: Argentine Army. *Informe Oficial del Ejercito Argentino Tomo II -Conflicto Malvinas* (Buenos Aires-Argentina: Estado Mayor General del Ejercito Argentino 1983): Annex 79.

Appendix IV– Different Perceptions of the Malvinas Conflict

Aspect	Argentina	Great Britain
Discovery	1502 by Portuguese Americo Vespucio. 1520 by Spaniard Hernando Magallanes.	1592 by Englishman John Davis
1833 British action	Great Britain invades and takes by force the Malvinas islands.	Exercised full and undoubted right over the Islands.
Rights over the Islands	Self determination of Argentine people. Population of Malvinas is inserted and not native. Sovereignty -*Utti Posidetis Iure*. End of Colonialism. Claimed persistently since 1833.	Self determination of Falklands' people. Effective occupation since 1833.
War of 1982 view	Malvinas recovery.	Repelling an invasion of the Falkland Islands.
War in 1982 causes	British provocation of Argentine workers in Georgias incident. Sinking of the Cruiser *General Belgrano*.	Argentine invasion of the Falklands.
War of 1982 outcome	The military aspect ended but the conflict did not end.	The War ended the conflict.
United Nations resolutions	Accomplished all of them, except UN Resolution 502.	Accomplished only when it was convenient to interests.
The current situation and future	The claim has been in Argentina's Constitution since 1994.	Great Britain delivered a Constitution for the Falkland Islands in 2009.

Appendix V: Falklands Observed System - British Perspective

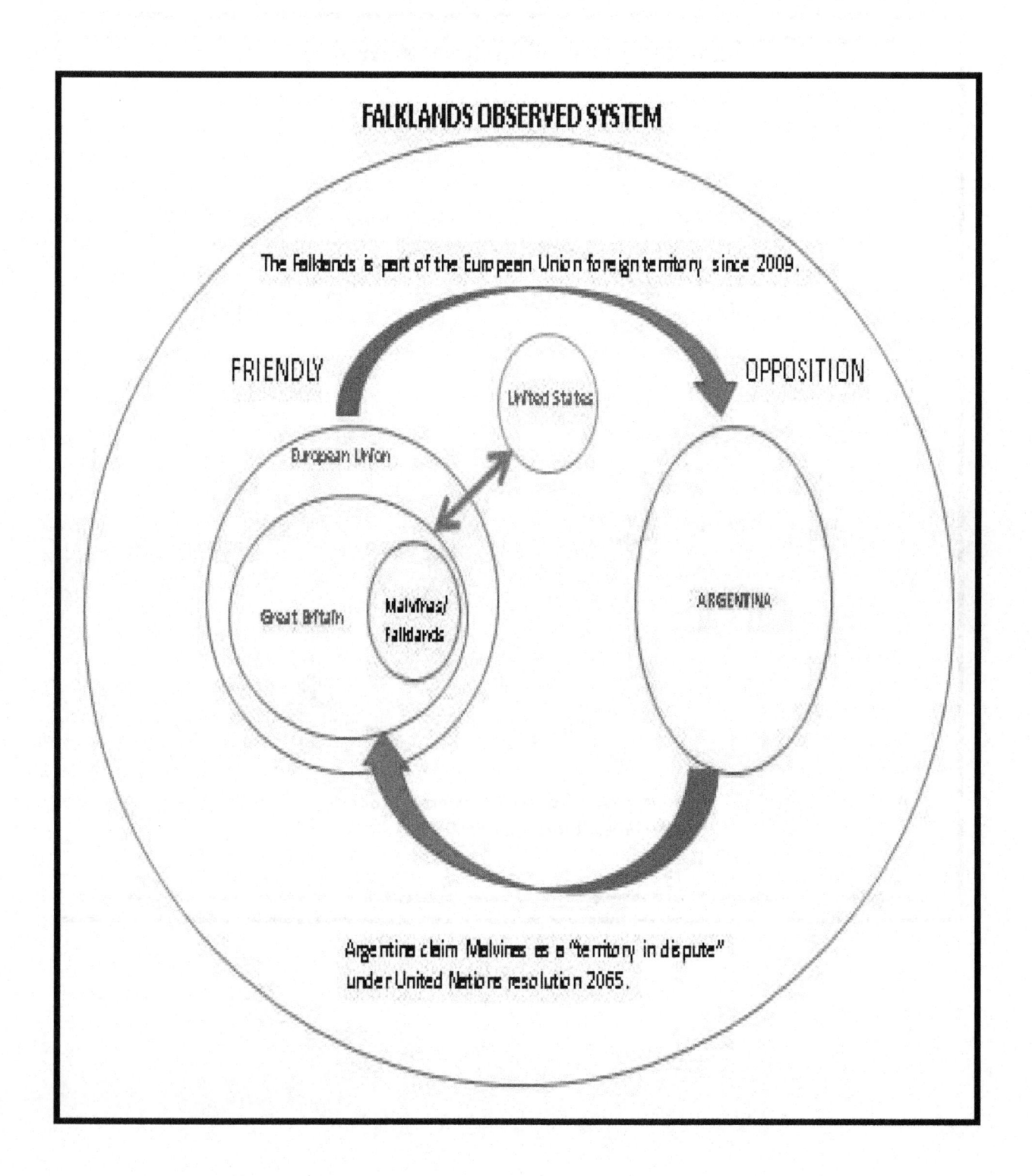

FALKLANDS OBSERVED SYSTEM

The Falklands is part of the European Union foreign territory since 2009.

FRIENDLY

OPPOSITION

United States

European Union

Great Britain

Malvinas/ Falklands

ARGENTINA

Argentina claim Malvinas as a "territory in dispute" under United Nations resolution 2065.

Appendix VI: System Propensity

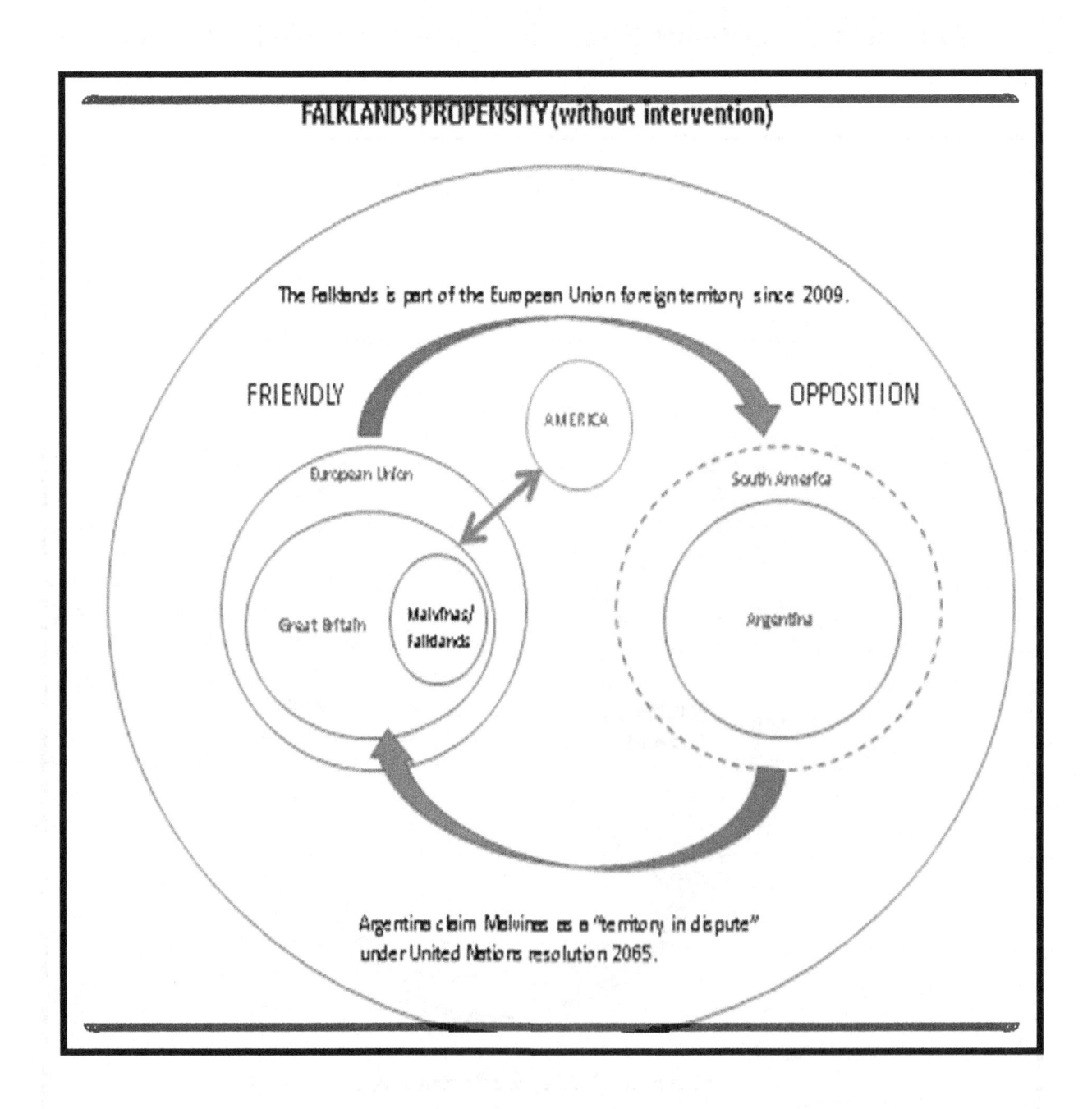

FALKLANDS PROPENSITY (without intervention)

The Falklands is part of the European Union foreign territory since 2009.

FRIENDLY — OPPOSITION

- European Union
  - Great Britain
  - Malvinas/Falklands
- AMERICA
- South America
  - Argentina

Argentina claim Malvinas as a "territory in dispute" under United Nations resolution 2065.

Appendix VII: System Potential (with Intervention).

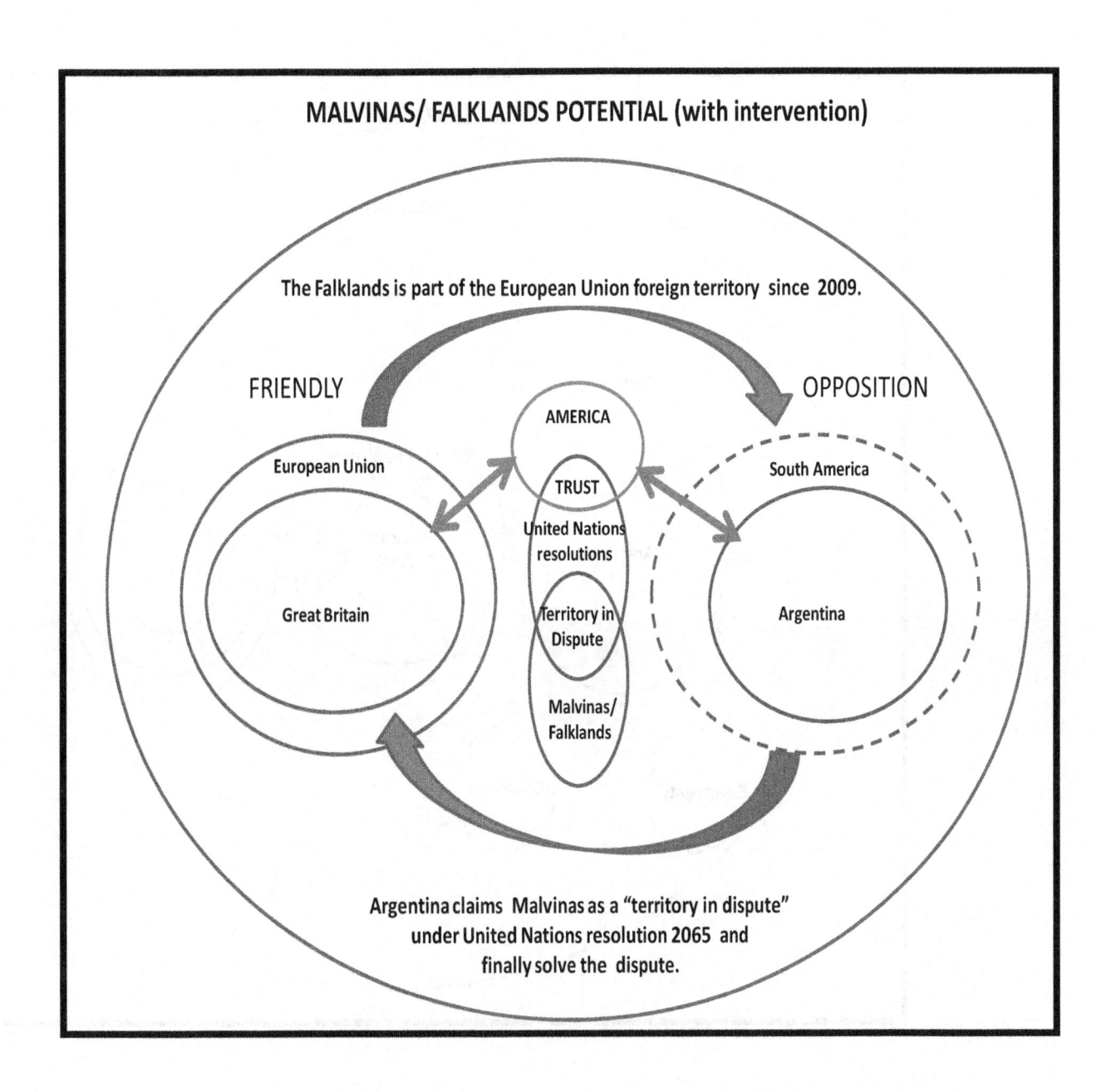

MALVINAS/ FALKLANDS POTENTIAL (with intervention)

The Falklands is part of the European Union foreign territory since 2009.

FRIENDLY

OPPOSITION

AMERICA

European Union

South America

TRUST

United Nations resolutions

Great Britain

Territory in Dispute

Argentina

Malvinas/ Falklands

Argentina claims Malvinas as a "territory in dispute" under United Nations resolution 2065 and finally solve the dispute.

Appendix VIII: Observed System- Argentine Perspective

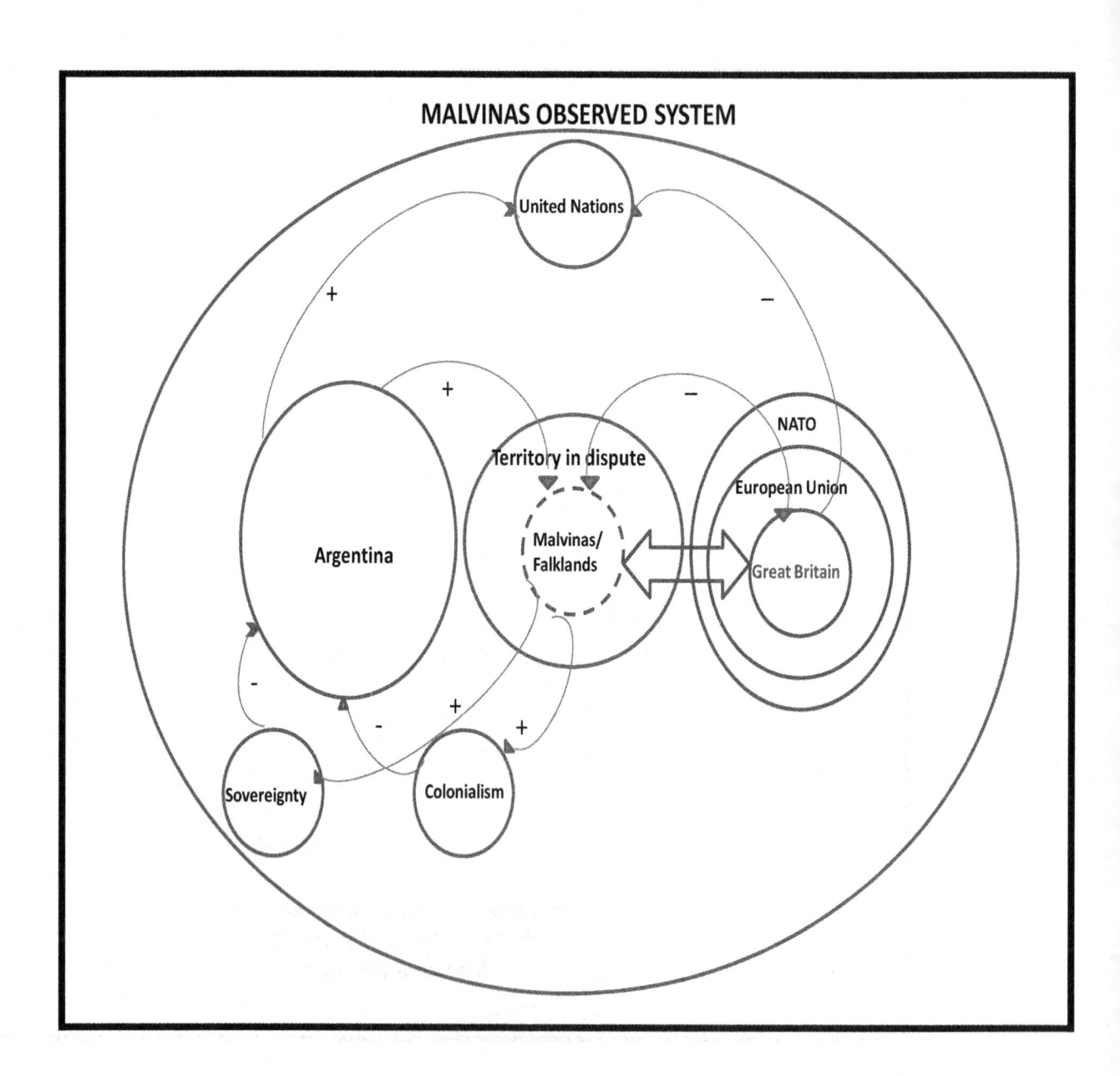

MALVINAS OBSERVED SYSTEM

- United Nations
- Argentina
- Territory in dispute
  - Malvinas/Falklands
- NATO
- European Union
- Great Britain
- Sovereignty
- Colonialism

Appendix IX: Tensions

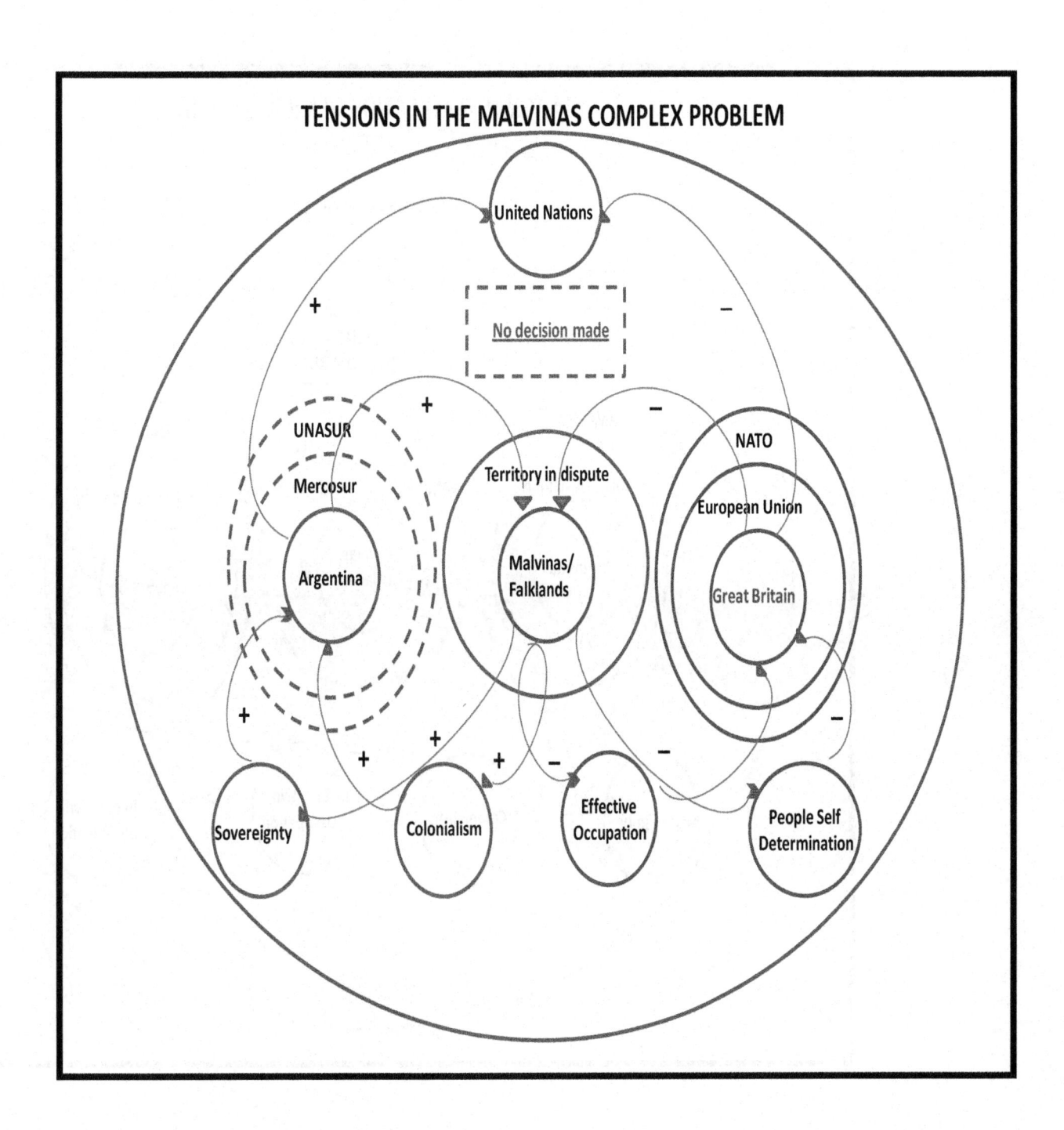

TENSIONS IN THE MALVINAS COMPLEX PROBLEM

Appendix X: Desired System

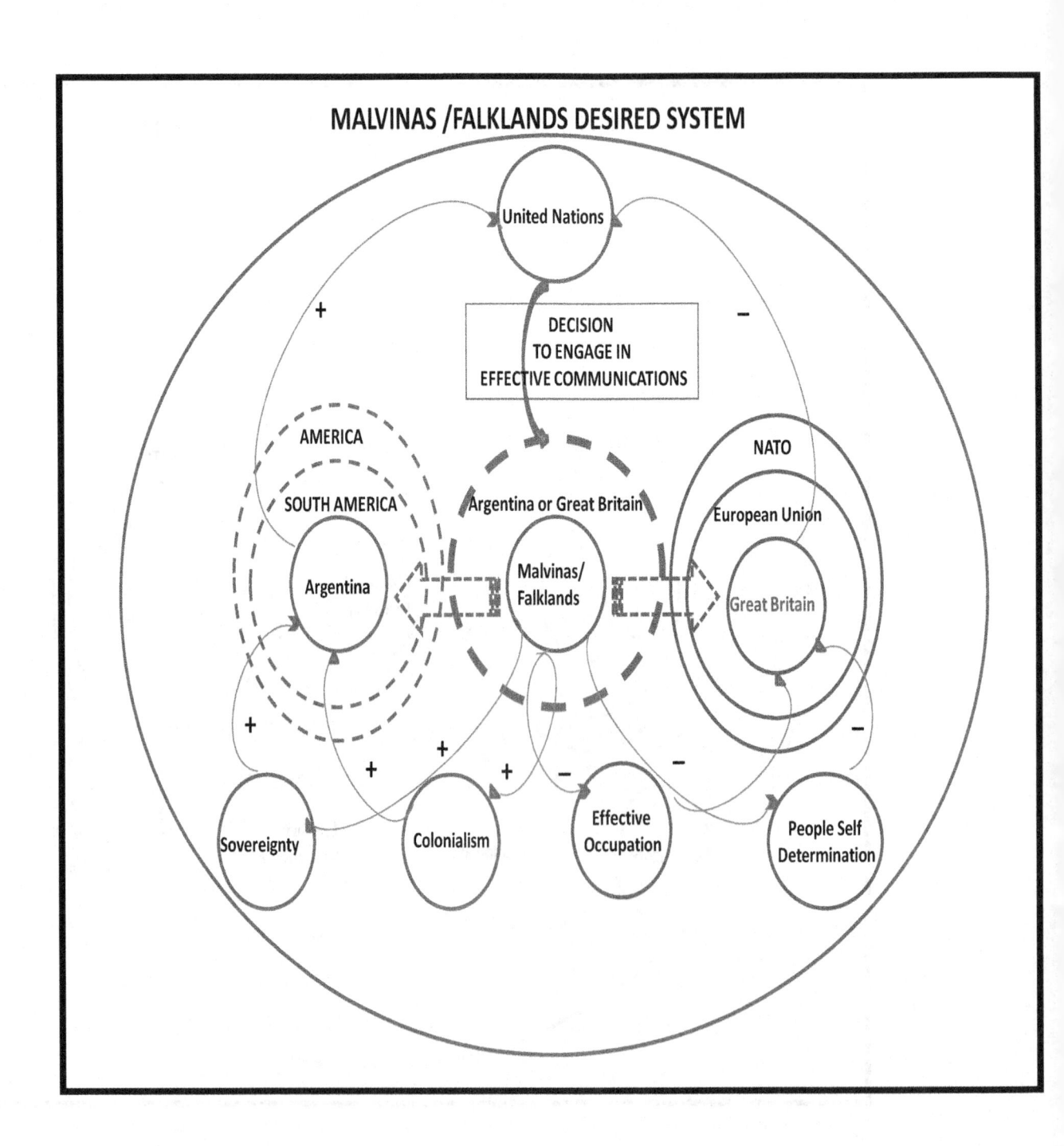

Guerra, Roger. *Political Perception and Political Miscalculations: Argentina's Role in the Malvinas War.* Miami: Thesis-PhD- University of Miami., 1990.

Gustafson, Lowell. *The Sovereignty Dispute over the Falkland (Malvinas) Islands* New York: Oxford University Press, 1988.

Hastings, Max and Simon Jenkins. *The Battle for the Falklands.* New York-London: WW Norton and Company, 1983.

Hoffmann, Fritz. Sovereignty in Dispute: The Falklands/Malvinas, 1493-1982. Boulder Colorado: Westview Press, 1984.

Jofre, Oscar. *Malvinas: La Defensa de Puerto Argentino.* Buenos Aires-Argentina: Circulo Militar 1990.

Landaburu, Carlos. *La Guerra de las Malvinas.* Buenos Aires-Argentina: Circulo Militar, 1989.

Makin, Guillermo. Argentine Approaches to the Falklands/Malvinas. *Was The Resort to Violence Forseeable?* (2001): 391-403.

Middlebrook, Martin. *The fight for the "Malvinas": The Argentine Forces in the Falklands War.* London: Penguin, 1990.

Moro, Ruben. The *History of the South Atlantic Conflict: The War for the Malvinas.* New York: Praeger, 1989.

Nye, Joseph. *Soft Power: The means to success in world Politics.* New York: Public Affairs, 2004

Owen, Bowcot. *United Kingdom Stakes Claim to Huge Area of South Atlantic Seabed.* 11 May 2009. http//www.guardian.co.uk/world/2009/may/11/uk-falklands-argentina-un (Accessed: 10 August 2009).

Ramphal Shridat, *Not Britain's Cause Alone: Address to the Commonwealth Press Union, 15 June, 1982* (London: Commonwealth Secretariat Library, Marlborough House, 1982).

Rattenbach, Benjamin. *Malvinas: Informe Rattenbach.* 16 September 1983. http://www.cescem.org.ar/informe_rattenbach/parte5_capitulo15_02.html (último acceso: 13 de August de 2009).

Robert, Booth. *Falkland Islanders Say Argentina is Waging Economic Warfare.* 14 June 2009. http://www.guardian.co.uk/uk/2009/jun/14/falklands-islands-argentina-economy-industry (último acceso: 10 de August de 2009).

Rodriguez Munoz, Chacho, and Luis Garasino. *Malvinas; Album de Campana.* Buenos Aires-Argentina: Fundacion Soldados, 1999.

Stewart, Nora. *Mates y Muchachos: Unity Cohesion in the Falklands/Malvinas War.* Washington-London: Brassey's, 1991.

Stuewe, Ronald Jr. "One Step Back, Two Steps Forward." Naval Postgraduate School. *An Analytical Framework for Airpower in Small Wars.* California- United States, 2006.

Thompson, Julian. *No Picnic*, London: Butler and Tanner, 1984.

White, Hayden, *The Content of the Form - Narrative Discourse and Historical Representation: The Question of Narrative in Contemporary Historical Theory* (John Hopkins University Press, Baltimore, London, 1987), 28.

Woodward, Sandy. *One Hundred Days: The Memoirs of the Falklands Battle Group Commander.* Annapolis: Naval Institute Press, 1997.

Bibliography

Aguiar, Roberto and Cervo Francisco, *Land Operations in Malvinas Islands*. Buenos Aires-Argentina: Circulo Militar, 1985.

Argentine Army, *Informe Oficial del Ejercito Argentino Tomo I -Conflicto Malvinas*. Buenos Aires-Argentina: Estado Mayor General del Ejercito Argentino, 1983.

Argentine Army,*Informe Oficial del Ejercito Argentino Tomo II -Conflicto Malvinas*. Buenos Aires-Argentina: Estado Mayor General del Ejercito Argentino, 1983.

Aulich, James. *Framing the Falklands War: Nationhood, Culture, and Identity*. Philadelphia: Milton Keynes-Open University Press, 1992.

Badsey, Stephen, R.P.W Havers, and Mark Grove, *The Falklands Conflict Twenty Years On: Lessons for the Future*. London-New York: Frank Cass, The Sandhurst Conference Series, 2005.

Balza, Martin. *AsiPpeleamos Malvinas: Testimonios de Veteranos del Ejercito*. Buenos Aires: Biblioteca del soldado, 1999.

Balza, Martin. *Malvinas: Relatos de Soldados*. Buenos Aires-Argentina: Circulo Militar, 1985.

Banach, Stephan and Alex Ryan "The Art of Design: A Design Methodology.". *Military Review*, (March-April 2009): 105-115.

Corizzo, Graciela. "La Fracasada Usurpacion de Puerto Deseado en 1670." In *Conflictos en el Atlantico Sur*, by Corizzo, Doval, Meli Ulises Muschetti, (Buenos Aires-Argentina: Circulo Militar, 1988), 27.

Circulo Militar, *Operaciones Terrestres en las Islas Malvinas*. Buenos Aires-Argentina: Circulo Militar, 1985.

Dorman, Andrew and Greg Kennedy, *War and Diplomacy: From World War I to the War on Terrorism*. . Washington D.C: Potomac Books Inc., 2008.

Duncan, Anderson. *The Falklands War, 1982*. London: Oxford, Osprey, 2002.

Evans Rob, Leigh David *"Falklands Warships carried Nuclear Weapons, MoD admits."* (http://www.guardian.co.uk/politics/2003/dec06/military.freedomofinformation/), accessed 10/25/2009.

Femenia, Nora. *National Identity in Times of Crisis: The Scripts of the Falklands-Malvinas War*. New York: Commack, N.Y: Nova Science Publishers, 1996.

Fernandez, Sergio, *Malvinas 1982: Symmetrical Misunderstandings and Overreactions Lead the Way to War*. United States Army War College Monograph, 2002.

Freedman, Lawrence. *The Official History of the Falklands Campaign*. London: Routledge, Taylor and Francis Group, 2005.

Gough, Barry. The *Falkland Islands/Malvinas: the Contest for the Empire in the South Atlantic*. London: Atlantic Highlands, 1992.

Government of the Falklands Islands. *The Falklands Island Government: People*. 2009. http://www.falklands.gov.fk//Falklands_Life.html (accessed: 13 August 2009).

Green, Gabriel V *Argentina's Tactical Aircraft Employment*. Air Command and General Staff College Monograph, (April 2005): 23-33.